Yes, God. Volume 3

Co-authored by:

Nicole Scott

Penne Allison

Jerri Haydon

Jade Stampley

Thessalonia Higgs

Karen Hernandez

JoEllen C. Delamatta

Moneshia R. Perkins

Cynthia Haymon

Gloria Berry

Yes, God. Volume 3
Real life stories of resilience, faith, strength, and trust

Copyright © 2023 by UImpact Publishing
All Rights Reserved

No part of this book may be used, reproduced, uploaded, stored or introduced into a retrieval system, or transmitted in any way or by any means (including electronic, mechanical, recording, or otherwise), without the prior written permission of the publisher, with the exception of brief quotations for written reviews or articles. No copying, uploading, or distribution of this book via the Internet is permissible.

The author, writers, and publisher have made every effort to include accurate information and website addresses in this work at the time of publication, and assume no responsibility for changes, omissions, inaccuracies, or errors that occur before or after publication. The publisher does not endorse or assume responsibility for the information, author, and writer websites, or third-party websites, or their content.

Yes, God: Volume 3
Real life stories of resilience, faith, strength, and trust

ISBN: 9798386523817

Saying YES is a choice.
It is a decision.
It is a daily walk.
What are you choosing to say YES GOD to today?

Table of Contents

Nicole Scott………………………………………. 6

Penne Allison……………………………………... 12

Jerri Haydon…………………………..………….. 28

Jade Stampley…………………………………….. 44

Thessalonia Higgs………..……………………… 60

Karen Hernandez………………..……………… 79

JoEllen C. Delamatta…………………………… 88

Moneshia R. Perkins………..…………………… 101

Cynthia Haymon………………………………… 109

Gloria Berry…..……………………………….... 121

Saying Yes to God is truly a faith walk and often it can feel alone, scary, exciting and just a mix of things. But as you read each story, my prayer is that you are challenged, encouraged, inspired, comforted and confident that you will find strength in your journey. Let's choose to walk with a hope and a sense of faith that what you are believing God for, He will hear and answer you.

Here's to Your Yes!

Kimberly DeShields-Spencer
Founder, UImpact
www.uimpact.net

Nicole Scott
Yes, God!

Each of us has a journey that God has taken us on. There are moments that occur along that journey that really helped to shape and define who we are. Share one of those Yes, God moments you have encountered, where you had to trust Him without knowing all the steps.

In 2018, I was walking and suddenly it felt like my leg was giving out underneath me. Later that night I felt the most unimaginable pain possible. Although it wasn't the worst pain I've ever had (I'm a Sickle Cell warrior). A few weeks went by, and I visited an orthopedist who told me a 48-year-old woman that my left hip had a condition known as avascular necrosis aka "bone death." He said I would eventually need a total hip replacement but not right away. That was June 2018. Fast forward to January 2019, the pain had intensified to the point that I'm having to use a walking cane.

My husband and I went to seek a second opinion. Well guess what? My hip was significantly worse. After much research, consideration, and prayer we decided that "eventually " was now. I scheduled the surgery with the original specialist for June 10. Some people do not believe that God gives us signs as to what His will is for our lives. I can tell you that He absolutely does! The problem is we don't always pay attention to those signs. God gave me multiple signs that this doctor did not have my best interest in mind, but I knew best, right? WRONG! One problem that I will expound on is my surgery was scheduled at a surgery center not a hospital that ended up being outside my insurance network. My husband and I went to the center on

June 10, but the team wasn't able to access my medical port to start the IV. The surgeon came in and said we would have to reschedule. To say that I was crushed would be an understatement. Then God showed me all the ways He had been protecting me in this process. Once I got over my pity party, I went to my insurance website and found the top Orthopedic surgeon in the area. She was on vacation, but I was willing to wait. My husband and I went to my appointment, and she listened and addressed all our concerns. This experience taught me that God wants me to always trust Him and to pay attention to his warning signs.

How did you develop your faith when it seemed like nothing was going right in your life? Share a situation where you had to develop your faith walk.

Faith means trusting God no matter what. It seems simple enough right, but it's really hard. Here's a good analogy -we trust that when we sit down on a chair that it is going to support us without question. When we have an illness or situation, we ask a million questions and do not immediately show our faith in the one who already has the answers. This is where I had to develop my faith and continually do faith checkups while dealing with a chronic illness.

Being diagnosed with a chronic illness and having a child diagnosed with the same illness gives you no other choice but to develop your faith. I can remember when my youngest would get sick and we would have to rush to the ER, I would pray that he wasn't experiencing any of the Sickle Cell pain that I know all too well.

How did you stay motivated in season where patience, faith and trust had to be exercised?

Years ago, I read that patience is a byproduct of tribulation. So, I immediately stopped asking for and asking others to stop praying for patience for me. A huge motivator for me is Isaiah 40:31- "But they that wait upon the Lord shall renew their strength; they shall mount up with wings as eagles; they shall run, and not be weary; and they shall walk, and not faint" (Isa. 40:31).

Waiting is not easy, and I honestly can not say it's a skill that I have mastered. I'm not sure I'll ever master what it means to wait, but that's also the beauty of it. We grow when we wait.

There were times when I still had to have my "pity" moment, but then I would not allow myself to stay in that moment. God says in His word that if I abide in Him, He will abide in me. He will never leave me nor forsake me. Sometimes troubles and crises come to remind me exactly who He is and that I am nothing without Him.

How did I stay motivated and how do I remain motivated- prayer, family, and self-confidence. I can not expect others to be confident in me if I'm not confident in myself.

What scriptures, books or resources do you recommend using when you are looking to grow in your walk with God?

Philippians 1:6, 4:19-God performs good works in the lives of believers. He promises to supply all of my needs.

Jeremiah 33:3-When we replaced the flooring in our house, I wrote this verse on the foundation at my front door. This verse is a reminder to my family that when we ask God questions, He will answer us.

Job 13:15-I really find life lessons in the entire book of Job. Job is stating in this verse that even though he didn't understand the reason for his suffering he still trusted God.

Matthew 17:20-21-One of my sisters in Christ quoted me these verses during one of my Sickle Cell crises. It serves as a reminder that a small amount of faith can yield big results. She told me to replace the word "mountain" with "Sickle Cell" each time I recited these verses.

Resources-a good Bible based Bible study that's focus is to study the word of God, other believers

Any last thoughts?

We run from places of discomfort when God really wants us to run into them. God gives all the opportunity to say yes. Writing this chapter has also been an exercise in saying "yes God." Initially I had doubts if I had a story others wanted to hear. Then I was completing a Bible study lesson and God clearly spoke to me and told me to shine my light l brighter so others to see. During the writing process this ugly stealer of joy attempted to rob me of completing this assignment by attacking my body with pain, but as I sit here typing these final thoughts, my heart cries out YES, GOD!

Nicole Scott

Nicole Scott has been married to her husband, Larry, for twenty seven years. They have two sons, Terrell and Jordan. She is a native of Arkansas, but Texas became the place she calls "home " nineteen years ago.

Nicole enjoys spending time with friends and family. She is very community, church, and volunteer oriented. Nicole serves in her church as a Sunday School teacher, a Vacation Bible School teacher, and a Children's Church teacher. She has served as an adult leader for Boy Scouts, band, orchestra, and class booster member. Nicole currently serves as President of the Garland ISD Council of PTAs.

Nicole received the MLK Drum Major for Service Award from President Obama in 2016. She received the Garland ISD Council of PTAs Volunteer of the year award in 2018. Nicole has also received various other recognitions for her service to the community.

Nicole earned a certificate in Women's Entrepreneurship from Cornell University in 2022. She currently works for an organization that teaches financial literacy to children, and she is also self-employed.

Penne Allison
Yes, God!

"The Dream Girl Journey" by Penne Allison

I have heard it said on more than one occasion that: "we live life looking forward, but we understand life looking back".

As I think back on my life, I can see how often the Sovereign Hand of God was at work in ways I could not see or understand. There were certain events unfolding. I see how God directed and redirected me, to be on the paths He knew I needed to be on. The journey I'm sharing with you now definitely falls into this category. I can point to a specific moment when it began. I can relate to you most of what has transpired since that time. However, the exciting and amazing part is that all the outcomes, results and manifestations haven't be realized just yet! My story is being played out in real time, and I'm so thankful and grateful to God that He allowed me to stay on the path despite the uncertainties and challenges I encountered. I'm so glad that my "yes" to Him, even when it was faltering and weak was enough for God to use me for His purposes and to bring glory to Himself.

Several years ago, and at a critical time in my life, God absolutely overwhelmed me with a strong impression to "engage women in weekend gatherings designed to help them pursue their God-given dreams." Something about inviting women to dream with God made my heart sing! There were several practical realities and challenges I faced which had the potential to drown out that song in my heart. One was my workload in the marketplace. I was the Nursing Director of a Level 1 Trauma Center with 24-hour, 365-day responsibility. Day-to-day duties required so much of me.

Even before considering the added pressure of leading my work team through the construction of a new, multi-million-dollar emergency department. Ten-to-twelve-hour workdays, five days a week, was typical for me. I was also a wife and mother of a pre-teen son. I was stretched. Our family was already engaged in a local church. My plate was already full. Why would God impress upon me to entertain saying "yes" to anything else, let alone this specific impression? Of course, I knew Jesus selected disciples who were already working on other things when He called them to follow him. They left the common place to experience the supernatural and to learn wisdom from the Son of God. So, I balanced my thoughts by reminding myself I wasn't one of Jesus' 12 disciples and acknowledging that I couldn't just completely ignore the impression that was burning strongly within me.

The impression came one morning while I was in my quiet place with God. This was the place I carved out special time, waited to hear from God and would journal. I would always write what I believed God was speaking to me. I had hosted a group of women for dinner the night before, where we came together to discuss how God wanted to help us move toward His purposes for our lives. The night was so sweet. We sensed the very presence of God. There was still a lingering of God's presence the next morning and my heart was open! I could sense God wanted me to think about the hopelessness many women experience when their dreams take a back seat to all the priorities in their lives. As I pondered and prayed, I got an inspired download. God gave me the titles of the sessions that could serve as a framework for a weekend event for women. I quickly jotted them down in my journal. The session titles looked wonderful, but where was the content? What was I supposed to do with this? My mind went back and forth on what to do for days as I thought about it. However, I didn't act on it right away. In fact, I put this precious inspirational message on the shelf for one year. Part of the reason for my inaction was because of my already full plate and I had accepted a new appointment to a church leadership position. Accepting this position created a stronger demand on my time.

After completing the one-year commitment in the church leadership position, I picked up where I left off a year earlier. I began asking God what he wanted me to do with the revelation He had inspired a year earlier. I prayed, I picked up the journal with the sessions and began developing a curriculum. God was so faithful; He gave me a second chance to say yes to the work He was calling me to do. I did not know at the time this work was part of my destiny and would shape how I view the importance of my role in the lives of women.

Since my schedule was so full, I had to develop the sessions early in the morning, late at night, and on weekends. God gave me specific objectives for each session. I worked on this for five months. Once the curriculum was developed and the sessions had some solid structure, I had a tremendous sense of relief. I had a vision of what the "Dream Girl Retreat," (yes, it had a name now), would look like, but felt I needed to pray over it with some trusted friends. I gathered a group of women to share the vision and to pray over the idea. This group of women agreed to meet weekly for six weeks. I wanted them to help me discern what direction to go in with this newfound revelation. After the six weeks of intercessory prayer, God wanted me to move forward with convening women to dream. During that season of prayer, I had a sense of urgency and a deepening desire to encourage women to dream.

I moved forward by securing a venue to host the weekend Dream Girl Retreat. I gave the intercessors brochures describing the upcoming event. The weekend retreat was advertised by word of mouth. On the day of the event seventy (70!) women showed up from all over the community. God showed up. As we shared information about Dream Killers, Our Identity in Christ, The Dream Giver, The Dream, Writing the Dream and Creating a Dream Girl Network, it really resonated with the women. The atmosphere was electric and pregnant with possibility. I felt like God had just birthed something great in me and in the lives of the women. It felt like a mountaintop experience. It happened when I said yes to God. God is so patient and kind even when we fumble around and put His idea in the deep freezer for a full year before acting on it.

Shortly after the initial Dream Girl Retreat Weekend, women asked me, "when is the next retreat?" They just assumed I would do another weekend retreat. My first thought was, I STILL have a full-time job running that same busy Level 1 Trauma Center, and it took everything within me to do this one. Despite the challenges I faced, I felt like my spirit was saying, I am willing, but my weary soul and groggy body are exhausted. I reluctantly returned to my daily full plate. Even though I went back to the mundane marketplace, I also longed for the exhilaration I felt that weekend. Once again, I put this work on the shelf but this time, I talked about it to whomever would listen.

As I look back now, I understand God is the God of the present. Savoring the mountain top experience could not be the end of the Dream Girl Movement. I hoped it was just the beginning. I wanted to facilitate more retreats, and regularly, but I didn't know how to make that happen. Once again, I felt like I was on a path that God placed me on. However, I didn't know, or couldn't clearly see, my next steps to move ahead on the pathway.

For the next few years, approximately five to be more accurate, I experienced an unusual season in my life. My focus and pursuit of the "next steps" for Dream Girls settled into a period of dormancy. The vision didn't die, nor did I lose interest in it. I kept my request for clarity before the Lord and shared the concept and initial retreat experience with many people that I met. There was no clear directive for action. So, I waited on God patiently (most of the time), expectantly while still believing God would give me His answer in His time. It wasn't always easy. I never had a great answer for the "when is the next retreat" question!

The most visible and tangible things that continued to develop during that season of waiting centered on family, ministry, and work. Our pre-teen son flew through his early teen years and was rapidly approaching high school graduation and preparing to head off to college. Making time to be available for him was a major priority and many experiences during that time are now lifelong cherished memories. Our church and ministry life remained active, and the pace at work never slowed down for me. We developed and enjoyed deep, close friendships with several friends in the area where we lived and did our best to stay closely connected with family all over the country. Overall, the

Dream Girl "Quiet Years" were enjoyable, fruitful, and productive. It just didn't offer the opportunity to move that ministry ahead.

Invisible to many people, God was building a solid foundation in me behind the scenes. I was growing my roots deeper by encouraging and engaging ladies I knew in their faith walk. Some needed a word of encouragement and prayer. Many sought me out and others were coincidental or even random encounters. Either way, there were many quality connections made, and I remained confident that my desire to minister to women was something God would use in His time. What I didn't fully realize, though, was how my "delay" in pursuing the dream God gave me would allow me to relate to many of the ladies I would subsequently share my journey with. A pivotal verse for me, Proverbs 13:12 (NLT), would take on a distinct and powerful meaning a few years later in my life because of that season of waiting.

Toward the end of this time, our family moved to a new city. My husband and I accepted new jobs and our son started college. Now, what once seemed like an amazing opportunity to do ministry with women looked as if it might fade away into the background. What was I supposed to do? How would I reignite the Dream Girl's fire in a new city nine hours away? We knew zero people outside of those we would work with.

Then one fateful day within just a few weeks of our relocation, I met a woman during parent orientation weekend for new students, as both of our sons were freshmen and lived 1 floor apart in the same dorm. It was a divine appointment! She and I clicked right away. My husband and I had meals with her and her husband the entire orientation weekend. We shared phone numbers and email addresses and began communicating immediately once we returned home. We became fast friends. As a result of the relocation, our families lived only about three hours apart as well, rather than the six hours' distance prior to our move. A few months later, I was in Atlanta at a nursing conference and less than an hour from my new friend. She visited me at my hotel for lunch. That day, I shared the Dream Girl Weekend Retreat experience with her. She immediately grasped the concept and embraced the vision. Within the next year, she had arranged for me to facilitate my second Dream Girl Retreat for the women's ministry at her church. Eighty-five women showed up and God showed up again. The atmosphere felt hopeful and charged with so much energy. It was amazing to see the second group of Dream Girls dream out loud. Whenever I said yes to God, He always showed up to put His hand on the event.

After that second retreat, my new friend said everything about the experience exceeded her expectations. She was a highly regarded and successful entertainment attorney who encouraged me to take the Dream Girl Retreat "on the road." She felt strongly that more women needed to experience the retreat. A few years earlier, she had an encounter with God that challenged her to help get faith-based organizations established. She was ready to do that with me. She, my sister and I met for a day of strategic planning at her house. With much prayer, we officially launched the Dream Girl Retreats a few months later in Memphis, TN and Atlanta, GA! As part of the launch, my book was birthed too; "I'm a Dream Girl: A Guide to Fulfilling Your God-Given Dreams." The Dream

Girl book was written to align with the content and curriculum created for the retreat sessions.

After the launch we enjoyed several fruitful years convening women in several cities across the Southeastern US. God showed great favor by opening doors to reach many women. This entire journey showed me how God was shaping my heart to continue helping women explore and birth the dreams God had put inside each of them. I had seen how God brought Ephesians 2:10 to life. "For we are God's Masterpiece. He has created us anew in Christ Jesus, so we can do good things he planned for us long ago." I felt like I was walking in the good works God had planned long before I understood this to be part of my purpose and destiny. It felt good to impart the concepts divinely inspired by God and to see women gladly receive a spirit of hope. Although I had spent many years in the marketplace as a leader in the nursing emergency department, I felt like God was changing me into a midwife in the spiritual realm. A midwife is a nurse who helps to assure a safe delivery. Birthing dreams into history may be harder than birthing natural babies because it often requires a change of mind. It is really hard work and there is no traditional gestational period.

Even though the retreats were going well, and there was favorable feedback and response to the I'm a Dream Girl book, I would sometimes have fleeting thoughts of self-doubt on whether they were making a difference. Would the women step out and go for their God-given dreams? When the retreats were over or when women completed a Dream Girl book study, I saw glimmers of hope in the eyes of hundreds of women. They were calling, texting, and emailing me to let me know their dream(s) had been started and many times had been fulfilled. Momentum was growing around this Dream Girl Movement.

I had just scheduled three Dream Girl retreats in close succession, instead of one at a time (intermittently) as had been done in the past, then the Covid-19 pandemic shut the entire world. The Dream Girl Retreats were no exception to the shutdown. I had to cancel three retreats in three different states. To say the air has been knocked out of my sail was an understatement. Here I was ready to take the Dream Girl Retreat to another level, only to face closing the retreats altogether. I was facing a real dilemma. As always, I began to pray and ask God what to do about this situation. I said yes in the past, but now I was feeling like God wanted me to say yes again, only this time I did not know how to move toward this yes. I was now isolated from the world in so many ways. The new pandemic status caused me to question myself and my call to minister to women. The more I reflected on this shutdown, the more I knew I could not move forward without giving God a total yes. A yes in the dark (pandemic) was a major faith walk. God had me right where he wanted me. A partial yes or a maybe would not suffice. I prayed alone and with other people during this time. I journaled a lot and got several ideas for writing new books at a later date.

God was doing a new thing in me. I could no longer rely on myself or even the people God put in place for support and encouragement. As I stepped into this new normal, I sensed God saw my faith and He could work with that. Even when I was feeling woefully inadequate, God reassured me through friends, prayers, and various scriptures. One scripture God revealed to me several times during the pandemic was Romans 15:13, "May the God of hope fill you with all joy and peace as you trust in him, so that you may overflow with hope by the power of the Holy Spirit." With so much hopelessness in the air, this verse was critical for me. This was a reminder that my trust in Him was indelibly linked to the hope that I so desperately needed in this new season. I had only known a Dream Girl journey that depended on in-person retreats and book reviews. God was now leading me to pivot from the previous approach to using new platforms. This was a scary place when you felt stuck in what you know. I was trying to show up with faith and hope, but doubt and concern continued to surface. I shared these concerns with my husband. He was very supportive and helped me learn the new platform, even though neither of us knew much about it. I also had a friend who was proficient at Facebook Live who agreed to be my behind-the-scenes hostess.

I launched a weekly Dream Girl Book Review on Facebook Live. This format was new and different to me. I was very uncomfortable. I didn't feel I was very good at engaging the screen. I was talking but did not see any faces, only comments in the chat. The new social media space was just not my cup of tea. I was not very familiar with the chat function as a host. I was way outside of my comfort zone. However, I saw new women engage in this platform I had never seen before. They seemed eager to meet me there each week. I could not completely see the big picture but sensed God moving in the background and moving me to where I needed to be. Each week, the momentum was building, and I knew I needed to continue the weekly chats. Once I finished the book review series, I started a different format for the Dream Girl Facebook Live. I interviewed women who had attended a past retreat or had read my book and were working toward their goals and fulfilling their dreams. These interviews resonated with the women. I believe they could see themselves in the stories my guests shared. They told of successes and failures and offered very practical recommendations to the viewers on how they dealt with their Dream Killers. Even though I was the host and interviewer, God allowed me to see His hand in this. If the difficulty of the pandemic had not happened, I would not have explored this new platform or these new presentation formats. I may have missed sharing these important stories with women who needed to be encouraged through the chat. To see guests' dreams coming true and knowing it was related to the Dream Girl message made my heart so happy.

God revealed to me He was making a difference in me and in other women who dream. I interviewed women who had started businesses, published books, recorded CD's, planted churches, completed college degrees, became seminary students, published blogs, and so many other amazing accomplishments. I began to see and appreciate how God was connecting many dots. When I said yes to God, I would be a midwife to many women. When I said yes to doing something different during the pandemic, He stepped in to show me again His Sovereign hand as I interviewed women week after week. It made me realize the dream God gave me had a multiplying effect. I had underestimated the power and impact of my yes.

All the Facebook Live interviews with the women were meaningful; however, one stands out. I interviewed a physician who attended one of my Dream Girl Retreats. She started a health blog after attending the Retreat. Her High School dream was to become a journalist at a major newspaper, but she was not even given the chance to be the school newspaper editor. The writing dream resurfaced and now her health blog is being read by many who are on a journey to good health. That chat by my physician friend was titled "Fulfill Your Dream with a Healthier You: A Chat About Weight Management." The goal was to encourage women to become healthy and stay healthy for life, making it a lifestyle change rather than a fad diet. The women were interested in the subject of weight loss. Many of the women on the chat were so engaged, we asked if they wanted to know more. We created an opportunity to gather via phone based on their enthusiastic response. A weekly phone call to discuss being healthier turned in to a support/ accountability group. Many of them joined the "Healthier You Dream Group" we started. We used the principles in my book of being in community and setting and reaching goals together. Some members lost 40-50 lbs of body weight and improved cholesterol numbers. For some, the progress was so significant their personal physician discontinued meds for diabetes. There were so many other success stories. Two years after launching this group, over 50 women have joined the Healthier You Dream Group to seek support, information, education, and unconditional love.

    The pandemic, at first, looked like the death of the Dream Girl Movement until God gave me another chance to say "Yes" to getting out of my comfort zone. Each day, I use a prayer app called Lectio 365 to gain strength and direction. I was part of an early morning prayer community called Upper Zoom that started during the pandemic. I was encouraged as I reread my book, preparing to lead the weekly Facebook Live Dream Girl Book Review. It reignited my dream to help other women's dream. Daily prayer and reading God's word allowed God to continue to speak to me and give me directions as to my next step on this journey. In addition, I read a few other books. One interesting book that stood out was entitled, "Fully You" by author Joel Malm. It was a book about identity. When you question who you are and what you are supposed to be doing, this book focuses on becoming the real you, strength in solitude, and the power of forgiveness.

I am currently planning for the first in-person Dream Girl Retreat since the pandemic. I am so excited to host women from 12 states (New Jersey, North Carolina, Louisiana, Florida, Pennsylvania, Texas, Michigan, Kentucky, Georgia, Arkansas, Tennessee, and Mississippi). Many of the women attending the retreat were a part of the Dream Girl Facebook Live Chats. This retreat, as with those in the past, will offer women a chance to begin a new walk with Christ and Dream Big Dreams. It will serve as a catalyst to believe God and never, ever give up.

Seeing God-given dreams come to pass even when they have been delayed, sidetracked, or interrupted truly gives me life. The Bible says, "Hope deferred makes the heart sick, but a dream fulfilled is a tree of life." Proverbs 13:12 NLT

Penne Allison
RN, BSN, MSOM

Penne is a dynamic, anointed speaker who has engaged audiences all over the United States including Harvard University. She received her Bachelor's Degree in Nursing from the University of Tennessee and her Masters from the University of Arkansas in Operations Management. She has been a nurse for over 35 years; specializing in Emergency Services. She has served in many capacities in Emergency Services (Vice-President, Director, Trauma Coordinator, Clinical Educator, Flight Nurse, Staff Nurse).

Penne has been a certified Nurse Executive who has spent many years overseeing operations of several Level 1 Trauma Centers. She has several publications in nursing and quality journals. Penne has been awarded leadership and excellence awards for her work with Emergency Departments.

She has been active in her faith community for many years, serving in various roles in her local church. Penne has spent many years teaching Bible studies, mentoring, developing curricula for women and other groups. God has given Penne a unique Women's curricula that is focused on calling people to walk in their purpose and pursue their God-given dreams. The Dream Girl Retreat empowers women to dream big, invite the Holy Spirit to lead, develop an action plan, and to be doers of the plan. Penne is the author of "I'm a Dream Girl: A Guide to Fulfilling Your God Given

Dreams." She has been married to Steve for 32 years and they have one adult son.

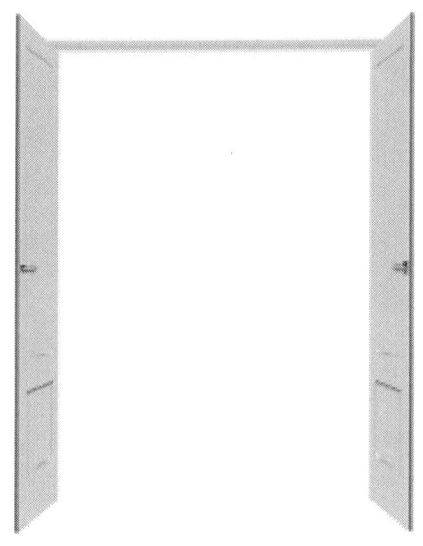

Jerri Haydon
Yes, God!

Each of us has a journey that God has taken us on. There are moments that occur along that journey that really helped to shape and define who we are. Share one of those Yes, God moments you have encountered, where you had to trust Him without knowing all the steps.

My journey of life has been full of Yes, God moments. To try and narrow this down to just one in my life for this chapter has been a tremendous challenge. My personal relationship with God began in my early twenties. Since then, the Yes God moments have helped me stay the course through the pits of my life. Oh, I've had storms in my life, but a pit is defined as a large hole in the ground and there were times in my life when I had to choose to stay in the pit or climb my way out. By climbing my way out, I mean the emotional, mental, physical and spiritual effort it took. Each of these works together to make my life whole.

God set the course for me as a young girl. My parents had always been very faithful in taking us to church. I recall sitting in church staring at all the beautiful window art, statues and Jesus our savior on the cross. I was amazed and captivated by the beauty of the inside of the church. I would try to imagine the story the artwork told and how much more there must be to all this beauty. Little did I know, Jesus was going to reveal to me there was and is a whole lot more.

Over my young adult years, I grew in my relationship with God, Jesus and the Holy Spirit. God is truly my source in life and my counselor in all matters. Whatever was going on in my life, it was God's council I sought first. It's always been difficult for me to share with others, but it comes so natural for me to share with God. Every morning consisted of a cup of coffee, my Bible and Jesus.

In the fall of 2004, I had gone to have a mammogram on a Thursday morning. After the mammogram, I headed to work and went about my day. Early the next morning, I received a phone call from the facility where I had gone. The woman on the phone asked me if I could report back first thing Monday morning. She shared that I should plan on spending more time there as I would be having another type of scan and also seeing a doctor for a procedure. As you can imagine, I was terrified. I asked questions, but the same response was offered for each question, "I'm so sorry, but you will know more after additional films are taken, and when the doctor speaks to you." I knew she was only following instructions, but I had to ask her how in the world I was supposed to wait all weekend for answers from a doctor. I let her know this was short of torture and I asked her if I have a tumor, can someone please just tell me. My efforts went unsuccessful. I assured her I would show up on Monday morning and we hung up.

The day seemed like it would never end, and I was hoping no one at the office could see the despair on my face. Internally I was in deep anguish and fought back tears throughout the day.

Although the phone call was not what I needed, God's timing could not have been more perfect. You see, this was also the weekend I had planned to attend a woman's faith conference with family, and it started after work on this day.

I met my mom, daughter, sister-in-law and niece at the conference. We checked in and went down for the kickoff of praise and worship and introductions of the speakers. I had not mentioned my phone call to anyone. I wanted the focus to be on receiving whatever God had for each of us. It did not need to be on me and knowing my family, it would have been. With laughter I'll add; our family is always in each other's business. This weekend I fully intended to soak up this time of fellowship and drawing near to the Lord. There is usually an abundance of wisdom and knowledge shared, and I was sincerely praying for a word or touch from God.

Near the end of the second day of the conference, I had gone up to join the women at the front for praise and worship. I had my hands open and was praying and singing. My eyes were closed, suddenly I felt the presence of someone circling me. I was not afraid; the presence of this person was very consoling. I kept my hands open and continued to pray and praise God. Unexpectedly there was a touch to my left shoulder. I never heard a voice, just a gentle touch of a hand to the back, the side and the front of my left shoulder.

I continued to pray and praise with hands open to receive. I put my head down and opened my eyes. I saw a light-colored denim skirt, black tights, and thick black penny loafer type shoes. I closed my eyes again and began to thank and worship God. I could feel the tears coming and I began to surrender and humble myself before the Lord. All the while, the women was still circling and touching various parts of my left shoulder.

There is no way to describe what I began to feel. It came on slowly and then like a fire through my left side and finally engulfing my entire body. This feeling was electrifying yet comforting. I became overwhelmed with unexplainable joy and began to sob uncontrollably. I fell to my knees with my face planted on my legs. I was experiencing what felt like lightning bolts shooting through my body. I have no idea how long this lasted but at some point, the woman had walked away, and I arose and went back to my seat.

The following night, my daughter and I went to drop my mom off at her house. While there, I decided to let them know I had to go in for a recall on a mammogram the next morning. As I expected, they were concerned and asked if they could go with me. I told them no, I wanted to do this alone.

Well, the next morning as I arrived at the facility, they were both standing at the entrance. We went in together and I was called back for my scan. Oddly, the receptionist allowed them to come back to the waiting area with me. It was at this point I felt my reason for being there was extremely serious.

After the scan, I joined my mom and daughter and we waited for what seemed like hours but realistically was only minutes. A radiologist appeared at the door and asked me to come back. He saw my family and asked if they were with me. I said yes and he said bring them back too because they need to see this.

We went into a small room and the radiologist placed a film on the board and switched the light on behind the film. He pointed to the film and said this is your left breast from Thursday and I've been doing this long enough to know what this is by sight. My eyes began filling with tears as I focused on a bulging mass with what appeared to be little spikes or mini lighting strikes coming from it. He then put up another film beside Thursday's film and said this is the film of your left breast today. He then pointed to the same area on the film just taken and there was no mass.

I wasn't sure what was happening and honestly, I felt a little in shock. He then asked me what I did over the weekend. I looked at my mom and daughter and then the radiologist and said I went to a woman's faith conference, and something happened. He said whatever it was you have something to be thankful for because someone is watching over you. I immediately said it was Jesus and hugged my mom and daughter. The radiologist said you are clear and free to go. We can't do a procedure if there is nothing there. He added be sure to keep doing whatever it is your doing.

Yes God! What I believe is that God removed a cancerous tumor from my body, and he used a woman, an angel, someone I will never know to pray over me. I was and continue to be forever grateful for this person allowing God to lead them to me. I don't believe God allows unfortunate things to happen in our lives. Life is just not perfect and does not always go the way we would like it to. What I want to make known, is through my sufferings, I have grown in my walk and seen the goodness of God shine through.

I would like to share that today; I find myself with a recent diagnosis of a positive malignancy in my right breast. I have no idea what steps I will have to go through, but I know for sure God will either take this cancer from my breast or the surgeon will. God can certainly do for me what he once did and remove this cancer. Will he? I have no idea, but if for some reason I must walk through this in its entirety; then without knowing the steps I must take, I will walk through this with hope and grace knowing God is with me.

For I know the plans I have for you, "declares the Lord," plans to prosper you and not to harm you, plans to give you hope and a future. Jeremiah 29:11 NIV

How did you develop your faith when it seemed like nothing was going right in your life? Share a situation where you had to develop your faith walk.

There was a time in my life when I felt like everything was closing in on me. Have you ever looked at someone and the way they were walking seemed like they were carrying the weight of their troubles on their shoulders? Well, I found myself feeling like that person. I could literally feel the weight of the situations in my life on my shoulders. You see, rather than give these to God, I had decided to carry these. Despite knowing God and having a personal relationship with Jesus, I began to question God. I would ask him if he was still here? Why do I feel this way God? How will you ever get me out of this mess God? In my alone times, I would cry out to God for help.

I was sinking in a pit and truth be told, I wanted to stay there. I did not want to come out and deal with the realities of my life. During this season of my life it was a daily challenge to step out in faith and walk the walk I knew I needed to walk with God. I had to have faith and trust that God would work things out for me, and that was difficult. Somehow God always managed to give me joy and remind me to give it all to him. I believe God does not intend for us to spend time trying to understand why some situations are as they appear to be.

Trust in the Lord with all your heart and lean not on your own understanding; in all your ways submit to him and he will make your paths straight. Proverbs 3: 5-6 NIV

Thinking back to the summer of 2005, it was just me and our two youngest sons living in the house we had owned for 18 years. Our oldest son and daughter had moved out and neither were making the best choices. My estranged husband was about to be away for a while, and although I had put our house up for sale, it was not selling. I had gone through the last amount of money we had saved. I finally understood that I was about to lose our home to foreclosure.

In the early summer weeks, there were many days when I felt like I was just treading water and getting nowhere. I was overwhelmed by the uncertainty of what to do about the house, worrying about my older children and the choices they were making, and of course the concern for our two younger sons and where we would live.

I had to focus on my job during the day and the evenings and weekends were spent going through each room clearing them out. Deciding what to keep and pack, what to donate, or sell, this was exhausting. I was continuously reminding myself, it's just stuff, or it's just a house. I would try to calm myself by thinking of others who might be going through something worse or more profonde. I would often say aloud, this too shall pass sayeth the Lord.

There were days when these thoughts would not last long. I would resort back to my thoughts of this was more than a house; it was our shelter for our boys. The home our older children grew up in. The home where there were so many first; times of joy and times of sorrow, it was our home. I was terrified of having to start over, and of course the credit issues that would play into this if the house were to be foreclosed on.

Trying to walk in faith was not easy. There were often family members surrounding us with love, but there were also those who would seize moments of our weakness to their advantage. I preferred to surround myself with the people offering encouraging words, or a helping hand. I came to the realization that most people wanted to have their voices heard. I just wanted the silence and some prayers. Too many voices were causing confusion and I needed to remember to stop and seek God's council. My daily prayer was to hear God speak or show me a sign for guidance. For him to open doors that needed to be open and close those that needed to be closed for me.

In this season, shame, anguish, and desperation were calling my name daily. I would try not to settle on the discouraging words some were speaking but instead on the encouraging words. There were life lessons that came from this for my family. We could see how words can be hurtful and once they are spoken, they can't be taken back.

Let your conversations be always full of grace, seasoned with salt, so that you may know how to answer everyone. Colossians 4:6 NIV

The waiting on God to move seemed like years. How in the world would God move in not just one situation but these situations? You see, since I came to know God, I have often found myself going through multiple situations at one time. God does not put this on me, it's just the way my life has been. Thankfully I have had him to lean on. I just had to turn my focus to him and trust that God is God and nothing is impossible for him.

Jesus looked at them and said, "With man this is impossible, but with God all things are possible." Matthew 19:26 NIV

End of summer was quickly approaching; school would be starting soon, our oldest son was living a very reckless life, and I was trying to find a way to get on a plane to fly with our daughter to Virginia; for which I had no money. Talk about the weight of the world. I was feeling it. I remember my dad saying to me "you've got to quit worrying about everyone and everything, or it is going to make you sick. You can't help what other people do or things that happen; you've got to help yourself first." His words helped shift my focus back on God.

He must have sensed that God does find a way to show himself to me. I was relieved when I got an unexpected phone call from my sister, and thankfully my family had put together the money to get my daughter and I on a flight to Virginia and then get me back home.

The stress of the house hadn't gone away, but before me and my daughter left for Virginia, I decided to take us out for pizza. We went to our favorite Fort Worth pizza place, Partons Pizza. We ate, laughed and had a good time. When we made it back to the house, I got the boys packed to go stay with grandparents while I was gone with our daughter.

Before we laid down for the night, I went outside and had a loud scream in the dark because I was heartbroken about my daughter moving so far away and so unexpectedly. Once I gathered my composure, I had asked the boys and my daughter to come to the living room of our home. I had everyone stand in a circle holding hands. I told them I was going to pray for our trip and the house.

I began by praying for safety and protection over our family, for the school year and especially for our daughter, and yes, even for my estranged husband. I closed our prayer with asking God to please bring a buyer for our house. I was specific in that I needed to get out of it without the house being foreclosed on. I added how nice it would be if God would please sell the house on or by August 15th. We said our amens and giggled a little. Seriously though, I had always heard to be specific in your prayers.

It was the morning of August 15, 2005. Still no buyer for the house. I was sitting at my desk full of sorrow and thousands of thoughts flooding through my mind. My cell phone rang, and it was my dad. He asked if I had a buyer yet and I told him no, still waiting. He said I know someone that mentioned to a friend you were selling your house and they gave him your number. He is going to call you this week. Shortly thereafter I had another call. It was a man letting me know he had gotten my number from a friend of my dad's. He asked if I had time to meet him today. I said the only time I have is during my lunch hour. He agreed to meet me for a quick walk through of our house.

Shazam, all praise and glory to God. How could I ever doubt him? The man made an offer and wrote me a check on the spot. God came through in a mighty way for me in this situation and of all days, the 15th of August. To this day, I am in awe of the power of God. It was difficult to have faith when I focused on the problem but focusing on God and his word made my faith walk more possible.

Some might call this a coincidence, but I am not a believer in coincidences. It's all about God moving for me. This was a situation my children bore witness to and agreed with me in prayer on. Innocent giggling because mom was asking God to help by a specific date, well apparently God does have a sense of humor.

I hope that my children will not forget this time in our lives and how the power of God moved in this situation. I hope they will remember how God pulled their mother out of that pit of desperation. The waiting was not easy, but it was well worth it.

But those who hope in the Lord will renew their strength. They will soar on wings like eagles; they will run and not grow weary, they will walk and not be faint. Isaiah 40:31 NIV

How did you stay motivated in season where patience, faith and trust had to be exercised?

It's not easy to stay motivated during some seasons of life. Depending on what is going on in our lives, it can sometimes be a struggle to exercise patience, faith and trust that God has everything under control. Staying encouraged by surrounding myself with people who will help encourage and speak life into me is a priority.

Saying short breath prayers throughout the day and a belief that God does want the best for me. Remembering and rejoicing in the prayers answered and the prayers unanswered. You see, some prayers aren't answered the way we would like them to be but know that at some point in life that prayer will resurface, and you will know why God chose to move in a different direction than what you prayed for.

I have not ever been very good at memorizing scriptures, but in the waiting, my Bible is a must have. God does not fail me; he leads me to a scripture that speaks to my heart and confirms that he is with me. I write these down or highlight and date the scripture. I find peace and rest by clinging to scriptures while I'm waiting and trusting God to work everything out.

I love worship music and playing worship music is always an opportunity to change the atmosphere wherever I am. Worship music is elevating and really helps to manifest peace and hope in my life. When our children were younger, mornings in our home would often start with worship music playing. I strongly believed the peace and hope I experienced through the music would spill over into their lives. To this day, in seasons when I need to stay motivated, it is in the worship that I gain supernatural strength.

If you have children, you may have discovered that they often have a natural insight to our emotions, regardless of how hard we might try to suppress these. My children may not have been aware of what they were experiencing, but they knew when things were off in our home. Keeping our family involved in church or gathering around the dining room table for scripture readings and talks helped to keep each of us grounded and motivated in seasons where patience, faith and trust are difficult. My youngest sons often express how they enjoyed the dining room table gatherings.

So do not fear, for I am with you; do not be dismayed, for I am your God. I will strengthen you and help you; I will uphold you with my righteous right hand. Isaiah 41:10

For I am the Lord your God who takes hold of your right hand and says to you, Do not fear; I will help you. Isaiah 41:13

What scriptures, books or resources do you recommend using when you are looking to grow in your walk with God?

There are so many resources and ways to grow in our walk with God. Recognize and take advantage of what gives you hope and keeps that fire burning between you and God. There will be seasons when you may feel like you're in a drought, but I promise, God is still with you.

There's no exact plan on how to grow in your walk with God. Do you, or you can find yourself completely overwhelmed. I find myself growing in my walk with God in many ways. I always have a Bible or a good devotional book within reach. Turning on worship music and lifting hands finding that place where it's just me and Jesus. Allowing the presence of the Holy Spirit to fill the atmosphere of my room, my car or even the shower. Long drives or walks outside just talking to Jesus and taking in the beauty of Our Heavenly Father's creations. As long as you invite God in, you will grow in your walk with him.

I can assure you that there is power as you grow in your walk with God and it's a continuous walk that is day by day. It won't be a perfect walk, but it will be an improved walk. You will find yourself stronger and more equipped to take on the daily battles of life. You may not realize the transformation happening, but you will also discover a new you.

I recently developed a new practice for myself. Take a pause throughout the day. Breathe in thankfulness, breath out be gratefulness. It's the little things in life that can be impactful and bring joy to your life. Be sure to let God know how grateful and thankful you are. He loves hearing how much we love him and how thankful we are to him. He deserves daily praise.

We are not all the same but my life experiences and relationships with others have shown me that whether you are a believer in God the Heavenly Father or not, God is with us, and he does speak and reveal himself to us as individuals in various ways. I have often heard, "God meets you where you are;" and with firsthand experience, I can attest that he does. He may come in little sprinkles, or he may come pouring out, but if you seek him, you will find him.

"So I say to you: Ask and it will be given to you; seek and you will find; knock and the door will be opened to you. Luke 11:9 NIV

For anyone who ask receives; the one who seeks finds; and to the one who knocks, the door will be opened. Luke 11:10 NIV

For God so loved the world that he gave his one and only Son, that whoever believes in him shall not perish but have eternal life. John 3:16 NIV

Jerri Haydon

Jerri Haydon is a wife, mother and GiGi. She has three sons and one daughter who is the sunshine of her life. When the Lord said multiple, that is truly what her children did. She is blessed with six grandsons and four granddaughters. This includes a daughter and grandson in Heaven. The heart and joy of Jerri's life are Jesus, her children and grandchildren. They truly rock her world. Although estranged from her husband for years, Jerri has been married for almost 40 years. They maintain communication and continue to pray for their family. Despite some heartaches and disappointments, Jerri considers her life to be so full that her cup runneth over. God is good.

Jerri enjoys spending time with her family and depending on the season, she looks forward to vacations to the beach and snowy mountains. She stands on Psalms 91 for her loved ones and verbally proclaims Psalms 27:13, I remain confident of this: I will see the goodness of the Lord in the land of the living. Adding including my children, grandchildren and generations to come.

Jerri was brought up by her parents with four siblings in Crowley, Texas. Her parents are very committed to their marriage and family. They instilled faith, unity and good work ethic in their children.

After several attempts at college, Jerri began a career in the non-clinical side of the medical field. Throughout her 35-year career she has had inspirational mentors and encouragement from her parents, physicians and coworkers. She credits these relationships and the grace of God for her promotions and accomplished career in Medical Administration. She acknowledges and give thanks to the

Lord for blessing her with her job because she never feels like she is reporting to work, but instead believes this to be an extension of the fruits in her life.

Jade Stampley
Yes, God!

In Matthew 4:19, Jesus gathers His disciples to follow Him. This scripture embodies Yes, God. When Jesus said to Simon Peter, and Andrew to "follow' Him, both Simon Peter and Andrew told Him "Yes." This scripture is profound. First, let's think about how Jesus *knew* who to call. He already knew who would say yes to Him, whilst knowing what they would endure. But because we know Him, we understand how He knew, this was no mistake. Second, the degree of trust Simon Peter and Andrew had in Jesus is commendable. These men had a surrendering spirit.

Share one of those Yes, God moments you have encountered, where you had to trust Him without knowing all the steps.

My "Yes, God" moment came when I did not consciously know I was saying "yes" with my next several moves. These actions, I realize in hindsight. It was in 2011 and I was a senior at Marquette. With graduating looming, I had gotten to a point where I knew I had to leave Milwaukee and provide a better life for my daughter. Thinking about it now, it seemed as if my thoughts of what to do and where to go were random. At the moment, they were. I do not know what provoked me to go to the campus library and begin researching for places to move. I just knew that once college was over, I needed to do more, and that I could not obtain more if I had never left Milwaukee.

My focus was to at least find somewhere that would garner my dreams of going to law school. My research was very short. I only looked into two states–Ohio and Texas. I do not know why I did not do more digging other than my graduation being around the corner, and I had to act fast.

During the Spring Break prior to graduation, I traveled to Texas and check out what all it offered. I packed up, then five-year-old Jaylah, and drove to Texas. What a wild, enjoyable, and frightening ride that was! I rushed to get Jaylah a portable DVD player to keep her occupied during the long drive, and we hit the road.

My main employment was working for Aldi grocery store. I thought, "what if I can transfer my job to Texas and work there first to keep stable?" That did not go as planned. I learned that if I were to transfer, I would not receive the same wage I was receiving in Milwaukee because of the cost-of-living difference. This was disheartening, but I had to keep trusting God. I know that when we have a legitimate thought and desire, making steps towards those desires shows to God that you trust Him. Therefore, I still moved to Texas in the hopes I could certainly find some type of employment until I can get on my feet and start making plans to continue my education. My, my my, didn't God laugh at my "plan."

After searching for apartments and enjoying my time in Texas with Jaylah sightseeing and melting in the 115-degree weather (2011 was HOT!), we made our way back home to Milwaukee. Once back home, I made the call to the apartment and could secure a place over the phone, signing the lease, and mailing in the deposit. You know, everything looks nice in the summer during the day, in most places. But to know that the apartment I selected was in a poor neighborhood was devastating once we finally moved to Texas. Nonetheless, I kept moving along, trying to figure it out. I was open to anything to provide for Jaylah and to live. I took any job to make ends meet.

Over the first few years, I was living, enjoying experiencing different things with my daughter, and even making way with taking the law school admissions exam. I would sign myself up for practice courses to take the exam, interview with different law schools, travel to different law schools for their open house events, anything and everything to accomplish my goals. At some point, my mother contacted me to reconcile our relationship. I was hopeful that she would be true to her word about wanting to move to Texas to be close to me and help me with Jaylah while I continued to follow my dreams. I was naïve. I should have let history tell me that this would not be a good idea. Even in Milwaukee, my mother and I had a tumultuous relationship. This was because of the emotional and psychological abuse I endured growing up. Things were bad for me and hard for me to understand. I always asked myself why she did not love me. So, the hope of reconciling and feeling loved was the motivator for agreeing with her that she too should move here.

Eventually, my mother moves to Texas. The plan was for us to live together. I later learn that this was a ploy, and I was manipulated into paying part of her security deposit for a home – I thought was meant for all of us. That was not the case. Before her move, I was told that she needed help with the security deposit, and I was to transfer the portion. Well, I already had my apartment with my own bills to pay. I had to make a decision. Unfortunately, my only option was to not pay the rent at my apartment in order to give it to her. I did not see the issue with this at the time because the plan was for us to live together, so I would not need to worry about not paying rent at my apartment.

The night my mother arrived was a work night, I had gotten off work and Jaylah and I went to the new place to wait for her. It was really late at night when she arrived, after midnight. When she arrived, she wanted me to unload the truck that night. I asked her if it could wait, given that the truck was rented for a few days and that I was exhausted. She did not care. So, I helped her unload things from the truck. Not just boxes or stuff she might have needed right away, she wanted me to move furniture. As I grumbled and continued to move things, she became irate. This behavior was seen in the past as I was growing up, so I had become accustomed to her behavior and foul words being said to me. It was in college where I learned she was using drugs, abusing alcohol, and very unstable because of being bipolar. This is why her behavior was always overlooked by everyone in my family. I was always told, "well, that's just her, you know that's just how she is." Well, it got so bad that night that I cried myself to sleep. Blamed myself for believing there would be a change, allowing myself to put my daughter in a negative situation, and really losing sight of the fact that I was doing fine before all of this. The next morning, things got even worse. I noticed she looked like she had not slept at all since the previous night. This, again, was known behavior. However, she was still belligerent and irate. Calling me horrible names that no mother should say to or about their child. And again, this was typical in my life growing up. But I got to where I was not okay with her exhibiting these behaviors in front of my daughter. My mother ended up kicking me and my daughter out of the house, unprovoked.

Here we are again. I hated myself so much for believing that things had changed since I had moved so far away and that things would get better. I was horribly wrong. So, now where do I go and what do I do? I completely abandoned the apartment I had. This left Jaylah and me homeless. Suddenly, my world and hope came crashing down. How could I let myself get into this situation again with her, to where I would end up on the street? This happened in Milwaukee right before I was to start college. I should have known better. Yet, I allowed her to manipulate me and act like she cared, but she was just using me.

I had to figure out where we were going to go. We had nothing, nothing but our clothing. I prayed and cried and cried and prayed and found a shelter to go to. This shelter was a faith-based transitioning shelter for parents.

How did you develop your faith when it seemed like nothing was going right in your life?

Here was my hope again. I truly had to trust God to make a way for us because things looked so grim that I just wanted to give up. I thought about the fact that God lead me in my search for a place to go to that shelter. I am grateful for that. At the shelter, they made sure we had our own separate apartment, fully furnished, with groceries provided. They even held church services. This is where my faith developed. This place required me to take part in their financial literacy training. I could work and save while providing for my daughter. The program was so great, as it prepared you to transition into stability, find a place to live, and help you afford what was needed to get approved.

The realization that I had come so far to get pushed so far down to nothing from my mother really tested my faith. If it had not been for God speaking to me through my tears, depression, and anguish, I do not know where I'd be, but I knew that all good things come to those who trust Him. So, I had to keep trusting. I had to keep going, knowing that everything was going to be alright. The moment I stopped; I would tell God I did not trust His plan for my life. Continuing to be in His word and listen to what He was showing me in every decision only strengthened my faith. At this point in my life, my faith was nowhere as strong as I wanted it to be, but I was still on my journey. I had a coworker introduce me to a new church home, Oak Cliff Bible Fellowship. This church fed (and continues to feed) my soul from the very beginning. The more I attended, the more my faith grew. When we pay attention to what is really happening in our lives, we move differently. I increasingly became more motivated, more hopeful, and more satisfied with the way things were heading.

Fast forward, my daughter and I are now stable, and I finally returned to being focused on my goals. I knew that life had gotten in the way, and I had to do what was necessary, but I was still feeling like I was missing the mark. I decided it was time to get back on track and back into the legal field. I had a job working in subrogation. I took this job to get back acclimated with the field and learn Texas laws. I became pregnant with my son, Jacob, and things were still going well for us.

How did you stay motivated in season where patience, faith and trust had to be exercised?

My son was born premature, 1 pound, 1ounce. He had to remain in the NICU for a couple of months. Although these were tough times, taking care of Jaylah on my own, traveling to and from the hospital every night to the hospital, sleeping in the hospital, and still working, I was still happy. When my son could come home, he was diagnosed with chronic lung disease. He had to have continued oxygen at all times. He got stronger over the next couple of months; he was able to go off of the oxygen tanks and was headed to physical therapy for his physical development.

On May 6, 2015, on a what seemed to be a normal morning of me getting Jaylah and Jacob up and ready, I was feeding Jacob and noticed something was wrong. His stomach became enlarged suddenly and I panicked. I sent Jaylah on her way to the bus stop for school and called my job to say I had to take my son to the emergency room. I was moving so fast; I did not know what was going on or what to think, but I had to get him to the emergency room fast. While driving, my son was crying so much. I was speeding and making it to the hospital. Out of nowhere, he stops crying. I pull the car over and noticed he was not moving. I screamed this horrific, curdling scream I have ever made in my life. I was yelling for help! I was pulled over right in front of an elementary school. I took my son out of his car seat, laid him on the grass, and called 911. My son was not breathing. All the while this was going on, I noticed people running from the school over to me to see what was going on. The dispatcher was coaching me to do CPR over the phone. I am hysterical! It was like I was out of my body while watching myself perform CPR on my son. As I was doing this, there was milk coming out of his nose. Cannot explain how painful this was and is right now to relive this. A few moments go by, and the ambulance arrives. I they grab my son, and I am on the ground losing it. I hear chatter about how he didn't look so good, then he was stable, then to, they were going to Care Flight him to the nearest children's hospital.

At some point, an advocate arrived just before the ambulance was leaving and drove me to the hospital. When I get there, doctors were everywhere working on my son in the emergency surgery room. I am in there for some time until they ask me to step out. I was still thinking that he was going to be okay. Suddenly, I hear a doctor say there is nothing left they can do. I drop to the floor in disbelief. I go into the room, and they have stopped working on my baby. They take all of the vital machines off of him. I am frozen. I am heartbroken. On the inside, I am dying. A doctor grabs my baby and hands him to me, lifeless. This is the worst thing that could happen at in my life right now. Another out of body experience as I sit in the chair, holding my son and I can feel him getting colder. I just really wanted to die at this moment. I rock and rock back and forth until someone comes in and tells me it is time for them to take him.

I AM NUMB. Someone called a friend of mine from my job and she showed up and took me home. How was I going to tell Jaylah that her little brother passed away? Why did this happen? He was doing well. I remember he was supposed to have surgery, but that the doctors changed the date or something. My son aspirated (accidentally breathing in of food into the lungs). When Jaylah came home from school, I had to tell her. She cried. I was still crying. I remember little 9-year-old Jaylah telling me at that very moment, "it's okay ma, he is no longer hurting."

Days go by and I am really depressed. The will to do anything set in. I then had the task of planning a funeral. Being on autopilot is the best example I can give to explain how I was functioning. I ask my church to perform the service and put mine and my son's name on the church bulletin. After the service, I went into isolation and remained in this autopilot-depressive state. I still went to work, cared for Jaylah, but I was no good on the inside.

Being patient, keeping my faith, and continuing to trust God in this season of my life was just as hard as the event. I went through life just doing. I kept going to work, I kept going to church, through it all. I felt extremely alone at this point. Then, as God always does, He put it in someone's heart at church to reach out to me. Ms. DeAnna Brown. Ms. Brown called me one day, extending herself to be there for me. We met and she showed me the bulletin from the church that she had saved and circled my son's name under the bereavement section. Ms. Brown explained how she did not know why, but she circled it and was compelled to reach out to me. To this day, Ms. Brown has been there for me and a true spiritual mother in my life. When I seek His word in direction, Ms. Brown is who I call. She has prayed for me, prayed with me, and taught me the character of God and His unconditional love for me. This gave me hope.

I believe I had no other choice but to be patient. At the job I had, I felt less interested in what I was doing and felt compelled to continue to move forward. I quit my job and took a job at a law firm, moving away from being a paralegal doing subrogation, to back to what I know and enjoy the most, family law.

This is where my patience, faith, and trust in God were being exercised the most. While still dealing with the loss of my son, I worked hard to know everything. Learning the laws of Texas and civil procedure elevated me. I was determined to absorb everything and help other families. I was encouraged by meeting clients in their time of need and allowing them to vent and discuss with me their case and how they feel while going through their tough time in life as I worked their case. Not surprisingly, because God is amazing and knows *exactly* where we are in life, God sends a client to my office who is going through a divorce, and I come to learn that we attend the same church. I made it a point to pay attention to this moment in my life because that was a fulfilling experience. God will and does use you as a vessel to fulfill His purpose!

Many memorable events in my life occur this way. I encounter situations and people that move me in directions that has always led me back to Him. God makes it a point in my life to put me into certain situations where I can help someone in their time of need that turns out to be something I have already went through and experienced. We sometimes use the term coincidence, but I believe that there is no such thing. God knows what He is doing, we just miss it sometimes. I stayed motivated and prayed to stay ever so spiritually aware of what is happening and why it is happening. This takes an exorbitant amount of practice.

I moved through that law firm receiving promotion after promotion. Then, the Holy Spirit came to me again, and I felt compelled to move on to something else, something bigger. I moved on from that law firm to another firm that specialized in more than just family law. I now call it infiltrating. I went in, learned all about other areas of law. I now call this educating. After learning, growing and cultivating my expertise and managerial skills, I moved on. I now call this elevating. Years have gone by since my son's passing, and although I have my moments of sadness, I continue to stay grateful, thankful, and trust in Him. I began my journey to Texas with going to law school in mind, but God has thrusted me into my purpose. Law school is not out of the question, I am still moving forward and receiving everything God has called me to do. I am saying, "Yes, God!"

What scriptures, books or resources do you recommend to use when you are looking to grow in your walk with God?

It was no mistake, the emotional and psychological abuse I endured over the years with from mother, constantly feeling that I am alone, and unloved, losing my son, God has allowed these events in my life in order to mold according to His purpose – for His Glory. God will move you in and out and around situations and circumstances in order for His will to be done, and His will, will always be done! I truly believe that I had been called according to His purpose. I have endured for a reason.

The book of James talks about faith and endurance. God will give you the provision of endurance for your trials. Many of us have been through some kind of trial in our lives and if you have not, just keep on living. Trials are going to happen, but His grace and mercy is so sufficient, that it carries us through. Trials come to improve our endurance so that we can move on and get through the next trial. Trials mature us during our walk with God. The book of James encourages Christians to ask God for wisdom, and to ask in faith while in the midst of our trial. I would recommend reading James 1 for this lesson.

There are a lot of scriptures that get me through some rough times, but I do not always know where to go right away or where to start. For these times, I suggest getting a concordance. A Bible concordance an index of words in the Bible that lists words alphabetically and shows the scriptures that contain those words. This makes it easier to find the right scriptures to read for what you are needing. For example, you can look for the word "fear" and the concordance will show every instance in the Bible where fear is discussed.

Another source that I use that was given to me by Ms. Brown, is a book called "God's Promises for Your Every Need." This one is amazing! It is of a concordance, but it lists feelings, thoughts, and situations you may experience and leads you to several scriptures that discuss that very thing. For instance, one category is entitled, "What to Do When You Feel…" then is lists several emotions you may be feeling. So, I am feeling lonely or angry, I would go to that section and find that term, which will lead me to the pages with the related passages. This is a great go-to book! Lastly, I recommend daily devotionals. The one I use has all 365 days of the year and the devotional is broken into both morning and night. Great way to wake up and get your morning Word and end the night with an evening Word for that day.

Any last thoughts?

Looking back at my life, I can honestly say that God moved every piece and ordered my steps, even when my next step was unclear. It is by faith and His Grace, that I am where I am today. I am not finished walking, no one ever is. This journey will take me for the rest of my life. Every time I've contemplated doing something and going a certain direction has been because the Holy Spirit has intervened for me, God has spoken to me – through my thoughts and dreams, and I have made the choice to listen, and say, Yes, God.

Jade Stampley

Jade Stampley, is the CEO/Founder of Stampley Direct Paralegal Services, LLC. Her company provides legal support for attorneys and legal services to individuals who are in need of assistance while they navigate through their legal matters. Her main focus is Family Law (divorce, child custody, and child support), however, I have experience and am knowledgeable in other areas of law such as: wills, estate planning, civil litigation, business formation and much more.

Jade was born and raised in Milwaukee, WI and graduated from Marquette University with a double major in Criminology and Law Studies and Sociology. She is also fluent in Spanish. After undergrad, Jade moved to Texas to pursue her dreams of working in the legal field and becoming an attorney. While in Texas, Jade obtained a Master's Degree in Criminology and Executive Leadership.

Jade has always been passionate about helping others who are going through a tough time in their lives. Life has given her the capacity to be empathetic and sympathetic to all types of circumstances and situations. Jade value how others feel when they are going through their rough patch in life and can understand how people feel in their situation.

While building a brand, Jade contemplated about her time, talents, and treasures that God gave her for the purpose of her horizontal relationship with Him. She understands her purpose lies in exemplifying that horizontal and vertical relationship with the Lord, by serving others.

Jade's life revolves around Jaylah and her dog Whiskey. She enjoys rock climbing, horseback riding, taking Jaylah on trips, museums, and reading. On the rare chance she has to enjoy a little "me time," she enjoys self-care activities such as spa days and naps!

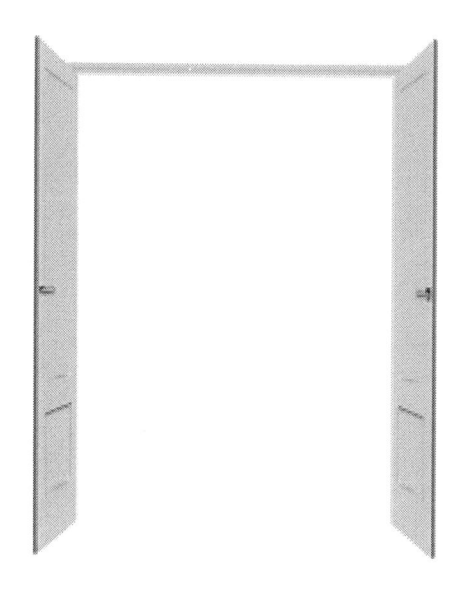

Thessalonia Higgs
Yes, God!

How did you develop your faith when it seemed like nothing was going right in your life? Share a situation where you had to develop your faith walk.

Wow, that's a great question. I have encountered many situations in life that has not only tested and developed my faith but also, rattled my life in such a way I silenced my faith for a while. It altered my mental and emotional state. However, over time and through it all, I learned how to grow and press through the pressures of battles in life. I will a few situations which caused my world to completely turn upside down, all while being engulfed by quicksand.

One Sunday morning on January 6, 2013, while in church at New Vision Christian Ministries International in Oceanside, California with my family enjoying Jesus, my phone kept ringing inside my purse. I reached down blindly to hit the ignore button several times. Suddenly, something didn't feel right. When my phone rang again, I looked at the screen and noticed it was my sister calling. Now, this sister never calls repeatedly, so I knew something was wrong. Therefore, I went into the lobby to answer. As she begins to speak, I sensed the distress and pain in her voice all while tears filled her speech. Instantly a quickened heartbeat overcame me as I listened in disbelief. My eye wells filled with tears, and I fell against the desk in the lobby. I felt like I was being choked because my breathing became extremely shallow. All, I could say was, no, no, no. Not mommy, not my mama.

At that moment one of the ministers was walking out into the lobby and noticed me in my broken state. I did my best to tell my sister on the phone I would call her back. At this point I didn't know what to do but I knew I had to pull it together. I had to relay this information to my younger sister who was in California with me.

Pause:

I will give you a little background history to explain why I am in California. I left home (Virginia) in September 2009 to become a United States Marine. After graduating bootcamp in South Carolina (2009) and completing Marine Combat Training in North Carolina (2010); I headed to Missouri to complete my military occupation training. Upon graduating there, I left the states heading to my first duty station in Okinawa, Japan. After, being in Japan for almost two years, my husband at the time and I conceived our first child. I didn't want to raise our baby in Japan, so I requested orders to leave. After speaking with my 1st Sgt. 'permission granted'. I sent my request in with my three choices (Quantico, Cherry Point, and Paris Island); however, none of them were available. I selected from the options they had available: Yuma, 29 Palms, and Camp Pendleton (the military likes to make us think we have a choice when we don't). Out of the three options they sent back I selected Camp Pendleton, where I lived for five years. I moved one of my younger sisters out to help me with childcare. If you don't know about childcare in California it is very expensive. It was a blessing having in-home childcare. Alright, back to it.

One thing the Corps taught me was how to adapt, overcome and keep it together when faced with adversity. So, I got up and pulled myself together and returned to the sanctuary to tell my sister. I shared with her that our mother and baby brother was in a very bad car accident two minutes from her house on the back road. Mommy hit a water pocket in the street and lost control of the vehicle. It was raining that day. She was on her way to take baby brother to work. Her van hydroplane and flipped multiple times, which is when she was ejected out the vehicle through the wind shield. When the van stopped flipping it landed on top of her.

While this is happening our baby brother was struck in the head with a mailbox that flew through the window. This knocked him out for a period. Once he regained consciousness, he undid his seat belt and crawled out the van. He found our mother with half of her body under the van headfirst. With the help of God, he was able to raise the van with one hand and pull her out with the other (crazy as this sound – in the face of adversity and with adrenalin we are capable of the unthinkable). Upon the arrival of EMS, they rushed her to MCV hospital in downtown Richmond. Our brother is fine, but mommy was not doing well due to the injuries she sustained.

As, I revealed this information to her, she immediately passed out and hit the floor. Then church service came to a complete halt. The pastor was informed of what just happened and everyone bum rushed heaven with prayers. Shortly after they finished praying for us we grabbed our things and left. When we got home, I called my sister back to have her contact the Red Cross. I need them to notify my chain of command and set up travel.

We were on the first flight out to Richmond, Virginia. At that time our second daughter was only a month and three days old and our oldest was eleven months old. My mind was all over the place. Yet, I prayed and prayed. On the flight I asked, God to allow my mother to pull through this. I needed her. We needed her. She could not leave us like this. This is unfair. I even said, "Father, with the level of my faith please allow her to return to her normal self once she gets through this. God, if you love me enough then you would honor my plea, my begging, my cry. Father please". I pleaded with God the entire flight. "I have the faith the size of a mustard seed and more. Will that be enough, God"?

Upon arriving to MCV hospital, I reached the Intensive Care Unit and gained access to see her. I was crumbling inside when I saw her laying there in that hospital bed. She had tubes all over. They placed her in a medically induced coma. They had shaved all her hair off because they had to do surgery on the left side of her brain. Also, they removed the left side of her skull bone due to the swelling. It was so hard to see her in that compacity. All I wanted was to see her smile again and hear her voice. I wanted her to see her new granddaughter. I just wanted my mother back. I prayed harder and harder for God to hear me.

I even begin to sing to her. I sung "Don't Do It Without Me" by Bishop Paul Morton. As I was singing my sister's MeMe and Casie joined in, out of nowhere our mother opened her eyes a couple times and silent tears slowly rolled down her face. At that moment there was hope and I knew God was doing something; or so, I thought. That was the final and last time I saw her beautiful brown eyes. I had to hold it together. I have always been known as the strong one in the family. The "go-to" person. I told myself I could not break, and I had to stay strong. However, inside I felt helpless with internal pains, all while being covered with sadness.

I had to leave her room. I went out and got some fresh air. When I returned upstairs suddenly, my newborn baby girl Eerah fell sick. I had to rush her down to pediatrics, only to find out she had bronchitis. Now, I must deal with my daughter being admitted to the hospital, my mother in ICU fighting for her life, and my brother on the observation unit. I said, "Lord, how much more could one person take"?

At that point my faith was not strong enough because everyone I cared about and loved was suffering in some way. I begin asking God, "what do I need to do for things to regain order"? I heard nothing. After a few days my daughter got better, my brother was released, yet mama was still fighting for her life. Then, the doctor pulled my sister's and I into the room to have "the talk". My sister's looked at me because they said, they wouldn't be able to pull the plug if need to. We spoke with the doctor for a long time and wanted to give it more time. Another week went by, and she was not doing well and started to have multiple organ failure.

I left and went to the chapel and spent time with God to tell Him I could not do this. I want my mother back. She is only 52 and still has a long life ahead of her. My younger siblings were still young. I was still active duty and had to return soon. I wanted things to go back to normal. Two weeks and a couple days passed, and the doctor called us back in to revisit the same previous conversation. For all to understand, it was the conversation to pull the plug on our mother or keep her on the machines because at this point the machines were doing all the work. My two sister's sat there with me and as we silently cried. They looked to me, and I said, ok. I felt at that moment God didn't care about me or my family because our mother was being taken away from us.

I felt at that time that I did something that caused Him to turn a deaf ear towards me. I was lost and confused. At that pivotal moment I became nothing but an operating body. On January 22, 2013, God called our wonderful Queen home. She received her earned crown of glory and took her rightful place with the Heavenly King. All her children survived her (starting from youngest to oldest): Monique Jones, Raydell Jones, Briggette Jones, Britney Jones, Whitney Jones, Samson Jones, Thessalonia Higgs, Trameca (MeMe) Clanton, Samuel Jones III, Casie Harris, and Teckela Green (stepdaughter).

After the funeral and making sure everything and everyone else was good. I returned home to Cali and my world was now shattered. I had no support from my husband, and I was away from family. My best friend/Marine sister Deshell supported me. My church family supported me. However, the one I needed the most never seemed concerned. I didn't know what to do. Now, I am broken with no mother, a newborn, a toddler, a broken marriage, active-duty Marine, full-time student, Director of the Children's Ministry, counselor, and still must be the rock for my family. What could someone do that wears so many hats? I was being pulled on from every angle.

I became so angry at God and wanted nothing to do with Him. I could not wrap my mind around His words, "No test or temptation that comes your way is beyond the course of what others have had to face. All you need to remember is that God will never let you down; he'll never let you be pushed past your limit; he'll always be there to help you come through it" (MSG) 1 Corinthians 10:13. During those moment I was trying to figure out, where was God? I felt alone in a valley and wanted to lay there and die. I thought to myself if God really loved me then, He wouldn't have taken so much away from me. I am not perfect, but I strived to do the best I could even in my mistakes.

I started to think, was this punishment? Is this the wrath of God? Here is why, to add insult to injury or to put fuel on the fire, as time pass by my husband started cheating on me. All of this is happening within a year of my mother passing. I still had not healed from everything else. I am saying, "what the heck, God? First, my mother, now my husband"? In tears, trying to figure out what I had done to deserve this. Now, what do I do when I tried to be the best wife I can; however, be told that "you are not good enough" or "you are fat and disgusting" or "I don't love you anymore". Yeah, that's Husband of the Year, words, right there. You see, I had developed strong and thick skin over the years from childhood on up. However, those words from him crushed me, and my identity left me. I never did anything to deserve that type of disrespect.

Ok, not only did I just lose my mother, but I was no longer any good to my husband because I gained weight while carrying his children. It was not even sloppy weight. I went from seven percent body fat and 143 pounds to 200 pounds (wore it well). That was after barring him two daughters back-to-back. He didn't even give me time to reset to do anything before he begin to mentally tear me apart. Then, I became nothing to him just that quick. The mental and verbal abuse distorted my very existence. I no longer knew who I was. I felt dead inside and worthless. Worst of all I could not call my mother to talk with her. As you can see one thing after another, over and over, so my faith was very minimal, at this point. My mother left me, my husband no longer wanted me, and God left me. That's how I felt at the time.

I am going to list the events to show you how fast my life unfolded and fell apart in a matter of years consistently. One event after another. Events as follows:

- 2011: had 1st child
- 2012: had 2nd child
- 2013: mother pass, favorite aunt pass, transitioning from military, husband cheats
- 2014-15: life is hell on earth (some good days but a lot of lost days), mental illness and loss of self-worth, martial separation
- 2016: godmother pass, starting divorce process, packed up and left Cali with my daughters and traveled about 3500 miles across country to Virginia in three days.
- 2017: tried dating and was physically abused and I attempted to commit suicide again for the third time
- 2018: forgave ex-husband and tried to reconcile for the sake of the family, had 3rd child and got remarried
- 2019: 9 mos. later he cheated again, but this time with is his deceased brother baby mother – left our family to marry her and father her four kids – divorced him a 2nd and final time
- 2020: both of my daughters start dealing with mental illness and spoke of suicide

- 2011 – Present: I have been suffering with life threating medical conditions, that the doctor tells me they have done all they can do. Yet, I live.

You see, I didn't have time to mentally process anything. I was at the end of my rope and all I wanted to do is die. I was literally the walking dead and life was obsolete to me. I wanted nothing and I meant nothing to do with God, but He would not let me go. I tried to take what was not mine, this life. This life was temporarily loan to me to fulfill His purpose and carryout His promises for my life. When I was a teenager, I tried to commit suicide by shooting myself, but God made it fail. I am 35, now. I snook into my parent's room and took their 38 revolver that held five rounds. I unloaded and reloaded to make sure it was loaded. I placed the gun to my temple and pulled the trigger. Nothing happened. I pulled the trigger again, but nothing happened. I unloaded and reloaded again. Pulled the trigger once more, that's right nothing happen. I was so angry. The reason I got to this point was because my father treated me different than my other siblings and went throughout the community telling people I was not his child. Why? because of the color of my skin. I was darker than my other siblings and I didn't look like them. Yet, I looked identical to my grandmother, his mother. For years, I went through life being the "black sheep." All I ever wanted was to be loved and accepted.

Anyhow, since the gun didn't work. I waited for about two weeks and planned to run my car into a tree on route 617 in the country. The day I was gunning for the tree God stepped in and blocked it. He caused my car to lose control right before I got close to the tree. That was the second time. Then, the last and final time was in 2017 when I was completely fed up and wanted to be with my mother after enduring everything. I was sitting on the couch in tears not saying a mumbling word. My oldest daughter Zaria (she was 6 at that time) walked up to me, wiped my face and spoke these words, "mom, don't leave, we need you". God will use a child to carry out his will. I cried even harder and hugged my little people and kissed them goodbye. However, I felt like I failed them and took blame for everything. I lost all faith and had no desire to pray anymore. So, I sent them to their auntie's house, and I returned home and wrote my farewell letter. I ingested 13 of my depression and anxiety pills, which totaled out to be over 10 thousand milligrams of medication.

Once again, God said no and caused this attempt to fail. I was ready to die but God had and has greater plans. He made the medication come out of every available releasing portal on my body. Then, when I looked in the mirror, I heard His voice ever so clear. He said, "I have need of you." From that moment, I vowed to never try to take God's vessel from Him again. I knew my babies needed me and God had need of me. That was one of the turning points for me. Even when my natural man wanted to ring the bell and throw in the towel, my spirit man rose and conquered. I will never live life aimlessly and reckless again. As time moved on, I begin spending time with God and trusting Him again. I started to develop my faith because without it I felt empty. By way of attending church, I was reminded that God will never let go. No, matter how much we try to push Him away. Yes, patience is a virtue and it's powerful,

In January 2020, I was set free. My life has never been the same again. I gave everything I had on me to the Lord and meant it. I was attending the police academy in Little

Rock, Arkansas. One weekend I went out to explore the area and stumbled upon a garden, called The Bernice Garden. As I was admiring the art and flowers, I looked up towards heaven, closed my eyes and took a deep breath. I felt my body jerk as if I just dropped a ton of bricks from my backpack. After taking my third deep breath, I opened my eyes, and my life was forever changed. I do not know what God did in me, through me, and for me; however, my life had never been the same since that day. For that I thank Him daily. Satan may be busy, but God is busier and will always win.

In my challenging moments I have develop a system for my life to operate in the 3P's: Problem, Process, and Promise. I am free because of my 3P system. I have learned to embrace every PROBLEM, while trusting God through the PROCESS, and allowing my faith to lead me to His PROMISE. After enduring everything up to this moment, my response to God was no longer, well, ummm, ok ok God. No, it became a solid and sold out 'Yes, God, where do you need me". There is no room for turning back. Now, my life is flowing with milk and honey because I look to see how God is building and leading.

How did you stay motivated in season where patience, faith and trust had to be exercised?

I realized the world can create trouble when things are peaceful, but I learned God can create peace in the mist of trouble. Also, I learned to understand that God have to keep His Word and promises to me. I begin to command Him to move because His Word (the Bible) said so. I begin to understand in life, that Satan does not want to mess with anyone that has nothing going on in their life. Because it's not worth his time. I have carried a mantel on my life that has been placed by God while I was in my mother's womb; therefore, that made me a threat to Satan before I was even born. The Bible tells us, God said before we were even born, God formed us and knew us, then He set us apart. I am led to believe since God knew about me before birth; therefore, Satan did too. I learned over the years to have patience with the attacks from the adversary. He only has enough power to do what I allow him too.

However, it takes time, sacrifices, learning to be obedient, tears, growing pains, daily faith work by studying the Word, continuous prayer and fasting, daily self-talks, counseling, mental reset (that truly takes daily training), failing, questions unto God, accountability with others, being committed to being uncomfortable so change could be birth, being consistent no matter what with positivity, and a strong support system. Again, daily prayer because anything birth outside of prayer is illegal.

I would have self-talks to really encourage myself. Whenever, something tried to arise, I would begin to speak opposite of what I felt. For example: When I felt depression trying to affect me. I tell myself, "I am not depressed"; "I am not broken"; "I am not defeated"; "I am not … fill in the blank". I believe whatever we say "I am" too, then, that's what we become. In return I would say to me, "I am healed"; "I am fearfully and wonderfully made by God"; "I am greater than what is trying to consume me"; "I will not stand and except what is beneath me"; "I am victorious"; etc. I would just begin to speak empowering and affirming statements to myself. After while I became what I spoke. I would redirect my focus on finding a solution, so that caused me to no longer focus on the problem itself. I told myself, I am its bigger supporter and fan. We are in this together and we are fighters, which has made me victorious.

I hands down trust God because He has proven Himself to be on time every time. Everything we encounter in life is not new; however, we often think we are the only ones. Learning to reach out when times are challenging is when you see your true strength and know you are not alone. We were never created to be alone, so we must stop allowing ourselves to become hermits when life hit us with curve ball after curve ball. I learned to connect with good Godly people that will tell me what I need to hear and not side with me to say what I want to hear. Lies and self-deceit will keep us in that dry place and going around the road every time.

Healing and change take time. I have learned to take everything one day at a time. When I cannot do that, then I operate in one moment at a time. Learning to find the hidden treasure in my problem is part of my healing and deliverance process. Oh, and "forgiveness" is key to our new beginning. It does not happen overnight. Therefore, as we allow ourselves to wholeheartedly forgive in time, we will see that being around that individual(s) or hearing their name doesn't affect us at all. That is when you know you have truly forgiven someone. It requires work, so we cannot be hard on ourselves.

There is nothing wrong with counseling, whether you are male or female. It does not make you look weak. What it does is make us a stronger and better person because we are able to step outside ourselves and seek help. It takes a real man or woman to, say "I need help", then begin seeking out resources. Remember, that is powerful. Always staying true to self. Trust God and trust His promise. No weapon formed is going to prosper because you are not giving life to it. I learned to breathe easy and ride out the storm. My soul is truly anchored in the Lord.

What scriptures, books or resources do you recommend using when you are looking to grow in your walk with God?

This what has helped me:

- Holy Bible:
  2 Corinthians 5:7 – We walk by faith and not by sight
- The Book of Esther: this book displays the power of obedience and blessings that come with being humble and having favor. She had favor in both her King (husband) eyes and The King of King eyes. Change if birth through prayer and fasting.
- 1 Thessalonians 5:16-18 – Rejoice always, pray without ceasing, in everything give thanks; for this is the will of God in Christ Jesus for you.
- Isaiah 41:10 – Fear not, for I am with you; Be not dismayed, for I am your God. I will strengthen you, yes, I will help you, I will uphold you with My righteous right hand.
- Psalms 27:1-2 – The Lord is my light and my salvation; who shall I fear? The Lord is the strength of my life; of whom shall I be afraid? When the wicked came against me to eat up my flesh, my enemies, and foes, they stumbled and fell.

- James 2:26: For as the body is without the spirit is dead, so faith without works is dead also.

- Discover The Hidden You: Dr. Myles Munroe
- Kingdom Woman: Tony Evans/Chrystal Evans Hurst
- Kingdom Man: Tony Evans
- Change Your Words, Change Your Life: Joyce Meyers
- The Shark and the Goldfish: Jon Gordon
- Purpose Driven Life: Rick Warren

Any last thoughts?

Learning to be comfortable being uncomfortable because that's when true change is birth. Only then can we truly embrace the change. Then, we must ask ourselves, "how bad do I want it because sacrifice will birth a shift to take place"? It's not easy being sold out for Christ but it is worth it. Anything that is lost in the growth, molding, and defining process, while return in abundance later. Stay the course for it has already be mapped. While we are going through let us focus on growing through, which will then allow us to see the reason we are in the situation, in the first place.

The power of ownership is key. We have the power to speak life or become stagnate. Learning to change our words will change our life as Joyce Meyers, simply wrote. Learning to be fearful of God enough that we desire to do things in excellence, which will impact our outcome. Lastly, I learned to be extremely thankful God closed some doors, didn't answer every prayer, and blocked certain opportunities. He knows best so it has become easier to trust Him, even when do not know what is happening nor is able to foresee the outcome. That is because I wholeheartedly, walk by faith and not by sight. I will live while I have the chance.

Thessalonia Higgs

I am an anointed and appointed Woman of God. Who has been changed, transformed, and set free. I am Thessalonia M. Higgs a Minster of God's Holy Word. I have been blessed to be the mother and nurturer of three wonderfully divine "little people". Who consist of two princesses: Zaria (10), Eerah (9), and a prince: Titus (3). I come from a little country town, Bumpass, Virginia. I am the middle child of eleven siblings who was birth by God's two most awesome individual's: Samuel B. Jones, Jr. and Pamela V. Jones. I have survived my beautiful virtuous mother. I am currently a Specialist in the Voluntary Service Department for the Department of Veterans Affairs in Richmond, Virginia. Where I also served as a Federal Law Enforcement Officer for a little over two and a half years. I am a United States Marine Corps Disabled Veteran. I served eight years in the Corps, four active and four reserved. My education accomplishments are as follows: Bachelor of Science in Social/Psychology from Park University; Associate of Science in Criminal Justice from ECPI University; nine classes left to take before I obtain my Master's in Theology from Liberty University. I love curling up in the corner of the couch reading intriguing books, sitting by the water, studying the Bible, spending time with family, shooting at the range, dining at nice restaurants, having one on ones with my little people, attending church, and working on my business. Through life trials and tribulations, I have grown to let go and trust God, even when I am blinded and confused. God never fails and His promises remains the same.

Karen Hernandez
Yes, God!

Each of us has a journey that God has taken us on. There are moments that occur along that journey that really helped to shape and define who we are. Share one of those Yes, God moments you have encountered, where you had to trust Him without knowing all the steps.

I learned to trust God in my Military career. As a teenager, I was confused about what I wanted to do for a career, so I joined the NJROTC at my High School Booker T Washington in Pensacola, Florida. Through this process I learned the basics. I took a swimming class as swimming/treading water was a requirement to join the Navy. I did everything that was asked of me, and I still could not swim or float. Upon completion of high school, I went to Navy boot camp in Orlando, Florida. I prayed and asked God if he would help me with this task.

When my company K002 had the assignment of swimming qualifications I was so nervous and again pleaded with God again to help me through this task because I did not know how I could pretend to swim, and I could not swim. Once I got into the pool, it was obvious that I could not swim and so I was sent to a separate area of the pool to learn how to float. After many mornings starting at 3:00am, I graduated to the 4-foot side of the pool. I was still nervous, and I was being advanced without floating or swimming.

One day I got to go into the five-foot section of the pool. I clearly was not ready for this task again I pleaded with God to help me through this situation because without this qualification I'm going to have to go back home with no direction. The instructor called me out of the 5-foot pool to the diving board to qualify. My soul froze as I walked to the diving area. Again, God please go into this water before me.

As I stood in a line of sixteen ladies, I tried to calm myself and I was doing a horrible job. All sixteen of the ladies were too afraid to jump and one by one I witnessed all of them being belittled and shamed by yelling and cursing. I said under my breath, Dear God if you are there, please be with me. As I approached the ladder, I heard "PEACE BE STILL" and I jumped in. My whole life flashed in front of me as I jumped off the diving board into the freezing water. My legs buckled as I hit the bottom. When I came back up, I was flailing for my life and the instructor told me to calm down and he placed his hand behind my neck and told me to relax. I was able to tread the water for five minutes with the angel instructor.

It was one of the moments that I will carry forever with me, and it reminds me that I am not alone and that I can always call on the Savior and he will show up for me. I constantly remind myself that he is always with me. I completed eight years in the United States Navy as IT Specialist calling on God in numerous situations where I did not see a way out, but he always sees me through.

How did you develop your faith when it seemed like nothing was going right in your life? Share a situation where you had to develop your faith walk.

When my mother fell and broke her hip on April 4, 2020, I was devastated. I was leaning on my faith that she would be fine after rehabilitation. My mother was a prayer warrior and had a much deeper relationship with God then I did. So, my thinking was that she is God's child, and we are all keeping the faith and praying constantly. My mother did not totally understand the whole corona virus situation. She was in rehab in a very nice facility that offered in-house dialysis, which was great. Our faith and comfort disappeared when the rehabilitation center told us that she was stable enough to be moved to a non-critical care facility.

My mother was a smoker so she chose a facility that would allow her to smoke in the courtyard. I looked up the reviews and I began to cry. The facility had so many bad reviews I could not believe they were able to maintain a license. Me and my family would talk to her daily and my sister would meet her as she waited for transportation back to the terrible place. We were getting calls from our mother stating that she had to go to the restroom and the staff was not responding. On many occasions we had to call the nurse's desk to get someone to her. My mother's dialysis port failed, and she had to have surgery. This surgery took over nine hours. The doctors tried going through her neck with no avail, they ultimately put the port in her right arm. Mother came out of surgery good and for a few days we thought God is on our side. She again had to go back to the rehab center.

One night the staff called to say they were taking her to the hospital, due to the port bleeding out. We prayed so hard, although our faith was wavering. The next day my sister when to the hospital to see our mother and she noticed that her mouth was crooked, and her words were slurred. The staff started to work on her. Once she was stable and back at the rehab the staff made the mistake of waking and dressing her improperly on the incorrect dialysis day. She said to me and my sister that she no longer wanted to do dialysis.

We asked her if she realized that without dialysis she would pass away. Her response was let me talk to God and get back to you guys. I lost hope and faith in this situation. Two days later, mother stated that the Lord said it was time for her to come home. My family banned together and took care of our mother, she lasted two weeks and passed away on August 10,2020. What restored my faith was knowing that it was my mother, and God's will to bring her to glory. My faith would never waver again. I understood that just because things didn't work the way I wanted, I would always have to have hope and faith beyond understanding. What my mother understood was something that strengthened my faith. I always try to see the good in situations such as the one above. She was tired from dialysis of nine years and she had many happy years here, serving God, her beloved church, and family.

How did you stay motivated in seasons where patience, faith and trust had to be exercised?

The way I stayed motivated in seasons where patience, faith and trust had to be exercised was I would read a lot of motivational speeches. I would keep myself in a positive mindset. I would always go to my Bible and read Psalms 121 where cometh my help and my help comes from the Lord so, I had to constantly remind myself that I was not alone and that things will work out in my favor. The roughest time was going through my separation and divorce. I had not been alone since my early 20s so this was challenging, I did not have patience with myself nor, I did not have any faith that my life could be better. I would have to catch myself so many times and remind myself of all the motivational readings that I had read and the Bible scriptures that would bring me back to a place of peace, faith and trust.

When the storms of life come and they do, I keep reminding myself to stay focused, and not lose patience, and not lose my faith. This was one of the lowest times in my life, being forced to ask God to please help me get my life back on track. I was suicidal and wanted nothing to do with this life. God showed me the faces of my three sons, and even though there are times when I don't see the value in my life, my sons show up and it lets me know that in any situation this too shall pass. I really loved running as a teen and walking as I got older. In July 2015 I was involved in a car accident, in which I had injuries to my neck and lower back. I had to have surgery on my neck because I could not feel my hands and arms.

To this day, I still have numbness in my hands and arms. I drop things all the time. I get depressed because I want to walk the way I used to and do the things I used to do but recovery is difficult. Therefore, I must always tell myself constantly tough times don't last, but tough people do. I used every day to learn from the previous day. I get excited for a new sweeper that will sweep like a vacuum and mop without bending or carrying heavy buckets. It's the small things that I thank God for that I can still do things for myself. It may take me longer now than before and that's ok. I realized that this is going to happen as we age and that I must fight each day doing the best with what physical abilities I have left.

What scriptures, books or resources do you recommend using when you are looking to grow in your walk with God?

I personally read my Bible and I have some friends who love bible trivia. I would take long walks with God which have become shorter since my accident. I now just sit in the sun and meditate with God. I like to journal and work on bible workbooks to understand better. I cherish the gospel musicians that pour inspiration and hope back into us when we are drained and feeling down. I watch biblical movies sometimes to remind me of the grace and mercy I have today. There are some books in the bible that really pick me up here they are as follows and the time it would take to read them. We devote so much time to everything else why not spend some quality time with God.

Psalms are my favorite. There is something for all of life's situations. This is about an hour. I love Psalms 121

1. I left my eyes up to the hills, where does my help come from? 2. My help comes from the Lord, the maker of heaven and earth. 3. He will not let your foot slip he who watches over you will not slumber; 4. indeed, he who watches over Israel would never slumber nor sleep. 5. The Lord watches over you the Lord is your shade at your right hand; 6. the sun will not harm you by day, nor the moon by night. 7. The Lord will keep you from all harm he will watch over your life; 8. the Lord will watch over your comings and your goings both now and forevermore.

Obadiah 4 minutes

As you read this book, remember that no one can fight against God's people and hope to win in the end the final victory belongs to Christ and his church.

Malachi 11 minutes

As you read this book, promise the Lord that you will not be complacent in your faith, but will put his will before your own concerns.

Philippians 14 minutes

As you read this book, remember always to rejoice in the Lord and to be content, whatever the circumstances.

Ruth 15 minutes

As you read this book, think about how God cares about you even when you sin and how wonderful it is that he sent Jesus, son of David into the world.

Song of Solomon 20 minutes

As you read this book, rejoice not only in the love that can exist between a man and woman, but also bask in the warmth of a personal love relationship with Christ.

Galatians 20 minutes

As you read this book, be sure that you are saved by a personal faith in Jesus, and ask God's spirit to help you walk in Christian love and peace.

Esther 30 minutes

As you read this book, think how God takes care of you in your everyday life, even making good come out of evil.

My final thoughts throughout this process has shown me my growth and I am excited to continue to do the things that keep me on a positive and learning note with God. Though we are not perfect we are given a chance every day to try again and to ask God to forgive us of our sins and to treat our neighbors and our families like We would want God would treat us. This is no easy task but the reward is priceless.

Karen Hernandez

I am Florida Native, US Navy Veteran, I have three adult sons. I'm a retired Telcom Engineer/Project Manager. I am not a Massage Therapist. I currently reside in West Central Florida.

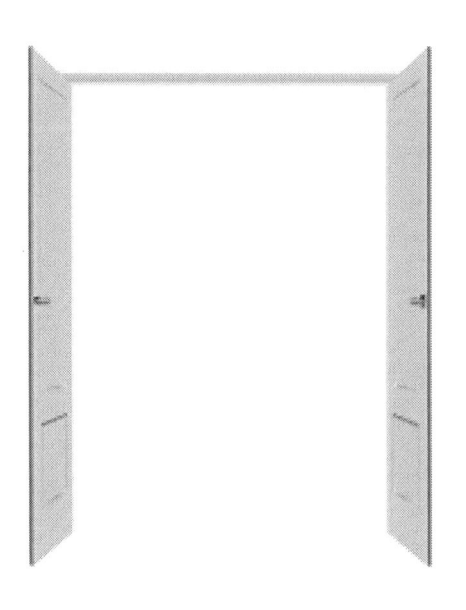

JoEllen C. Delamatta
Yes, God!

I said **Yes Lord** initially when I turned eight years old at a James Robison evangelistic campaign in my hometown of Hattiesburg, Mississippi. The next week I talked with my pastor, Elwood Nobles and he baptized me in the Black Creek River that same afternoon. This was always been a memorable experience since I got a head to toe rash from poison ivy from the water. However, one of the sweetest memories with my dad came as he cared for me during that two week healing period. He had recently become a Christian after a 25 year military career and service overseas. We were both learning about Jesus at the same time. What I didn't know at the time was that I would have only one more year with my earthly father as he was suffering from bone cancer.

Losing daddy has had a lifelong indention in who I am. The loss affected many relationships in my youth and adulthood. I often looked for a male counterpart to affirm me in what I did and whom I wanted to become. I am forever grateful to my one and only sibling, my older brother, who has ALWAYS been my friend and confidant and has stuck by me and supported me through many valleys and mountaintop experiences. It has been a long road to find the steadfast love of the Lord that never ceases. I was often looking in ALL the wrong places that the world was showing me.

Living at home during my first two years of college was a financial necessity but one that came with some bad choices as I looked to be affirmed and loved by someone of my choosing versus looking to the Lord. As I straddled the fence to wait for God's best, I would also seek to please those around me by busying myself in the church, yet not always listening to God's voice. I was involved in the church youth group, handbell choir, adult choir, summer missions' programs, and Baptist student union outreach. While these programs brought great interaction with Christian people, they did not always create a connection to the Father in heaven.

After high school, wanderlust grabbed me as I took my first solo trip to Europe with my Latin and Mythology teacher. (My family and I had lived in Izmir, Turkey for two years thanks to my dad's last tour as an Army Master Sergeant) Traveling with a group of students and adults to England, Switzerland, Greece, Crete, and Italy was simply tasting a whole new evidence of God's grace in what I had studied both at school and at church. Being able to see places that were mentioned in God's Word was amazing. For example, we went to Athens, where the apostle Paul spoke and noted the altar to the unknown god when he preached on Mars Hill in Acts 17. As a 19-year-old standing in the same space as Paul was a life altering moment. I recognized how God's Word could come alive if we don't just read it, but we take in the word and intentionally sup on its truth.

Upon graduation from Baylor University, I felt a tug at my heart to serve God in a faraway land. I was thinking Switzerland or Belgium, but God had another plan and chose a country in West Africa called Senegal. One hundred degree desert heat, flying bugs, and splendid smiles greeted me at the Dakar Yoff airport. I soon met Elizabeth who was a young pre-teen who was donning a pair of dusty crutches. A few years earlier, she wanted to end her poor and forlorn existence on the edge of the train tracks. God had a plan and when I met Elizabeth she began to express her joy that she had found in finding Jesus after the train. Her joy was contagious and enabled her to relate to so many girls and women who were distraught and unaware of God's grace. Amidst her frailty and self-induced disability, Jehovah God was changing her from the inside out with hope and perspective on how God reaches down to pull us from the mire. What a powerful vision of how Jehovah Jireh provides for His children in ways that I had never known. This was like in the book of Genesis with Abraham and the Lord providing a ram to be the sacrifice for his son Isaac.

Suma xarit, Mbaye, another young adult that I got to sing alongside in church in Thies, Senegal had come to a saving love of Jesus and adored the song 'Dan mon ame un beau soleil brille." This song explains that in my soul a beautiful warmth illuminates me. God used Mbaye in so many lives for such a short period of time on this earth. He used him to remind me and many others about the change and the joyful hope we have in the Creator God who loves us deeply. Mbaye was killed while on active duty in the Casamance where vigilantes were posted throughout the region. I was so broken in learning of his passing but knew that he was walking in the 'Kingdom come' and was a faithful servant all his days from the time he met Jesus his Savior. He is singing along with the angelic host as I remmeber his smile and sense the warmth of God's grace when I remember him. The lesson learned upon reflection was Mbaye's vigor in sharing the love of Jesus with everyone in his surroundings because he was filled up with God's love and joy and it was contagious. The scripture in Psalms 16 reminds me, 'in His presence there is fullness of joy' which carries me often in times of distress and exuberance.

From Senegal back to the USA, I was engaged to be married to a Frenchman whom I met while studying at Baylor. He came to learn about this West African nation where I was serving for a year, as we wrote daily letters to one another. After a few months I contracted a bad case of malaria. My fiancé came to check on me while I was in Senegal. Through high fevers, delirium, and many days of migraines and pain, God began to show us both what 'serving the Lord' was all about. This was a lesson of surrender far from the ease and comfort of family, facility with hospitals and medicine. We were learning to LEAN on God the Healer and Redeemer of our bodies and souls. This season caused me to ask: did I truly believe in Jehovah Rapha?

We continued to seek God's face for where and what He wanted from us both. Both D and I recognized the call to return and continue the work that had begun in this desert jewel.

After spending an academic year in Senegal and recovering from malaria, D and I were married and eventually became parents of three gorgeous girls.

Becoming a mother began my journey of surrender in a whole new way. It was suddenly and clearly NOT about me anymore. Like in the airplane spiel, putting your oxygen mask on before your child's gave me an incredible visual that I needed to always breathe in God's truth, read and implement His word, in order to be able to be what they needed of me and many others around me. His promise in Deuteronomy 31:6 says, " be strong and courageous and Do not be terrified …for the Lord your God goes with you. He will never leave us nor forsake you". This gave me strength when my physical strength failed.

The maternal surrender is not immediate but often incremental. As a baby's needs change and develops;, the ability to listen, learn, and discern expands in every mother and father. Every child is individually different and as I learned this with my three cherubs, I began to see the parallel relationship with my Father in heaven. I am not always receptive to what my Heavenly Father is teaching me which is why I often have to repeat the lesson that He is trying to show me. This is similar to my children not wanting to obey or listen to what they have been shown. God's word is truly a light to my path and His Spirit gives me glimpses of His grace. Currently my grown children are sowing into my life. What a treasured dividend to the investment made so many years ago.

Another moment of surrender came many years later when I was asked to teach in the Illubabor region of Ethiopia. This was about 12 hours south west of Addis Ababa. The opportunity to teach English as a native speaker to high school and college age students for four weeks, Monday through Friday for four hours daily, was a humbling experience. I listened to many students recount how they had walked from their villages for one, two and even four hours one way to reach the school in time for English class. These students were determined and dedicated to learn English from this teacher from America. Learning English would facilitate their possibilities of getting a higher score on the national exam in university level study This would later help them to gain lucrative work. Several years earlier, when my divorce seemed imminent, there was a pastor who prophesied over me sharing that I would someday preach and teach to a throbbing crowd, hundreds upon hundreds who were thirsting for truth. I had great incredulity in his words, but they never left me. Those words immediately resurfaced on the first Sunday after our arrival in the Illubabor Bethel Synod of Mettu, Ethiopia. About 15 minutes before the service was about to begin, one of the elders of the assembly where we were visiting came to me and asked if I would preach. Their pastor had to go to another church that very morning and needed a replacement. They understood from one of my colleagues that I had seminary training and the elders had prayed for God to answer this need. I was in shock and as I looked out over the congregation, under the canopy keeping us dry from the incessant rains, the church folk continued to flow in; mothers and their babies, older adults, children, and many parishioners. The overflow section began to fill too, and I asked the elder how many parishioners were typical for a Sunday morning service as this was a fairly new church within the town of Mettu. He said, "anywhere from 400-600 on any given Sunday, but there seems to be more today even with the relentless rain." God soon gave me a word from the text in Ezra. As I watched the women all in white gauze dresses, spun by their own cotton and sewn by the women's auxiliary of the church, I remembered the prophecy of the pastor years earlier. I began to weep. In that moment, I realized what God saw in me but I was too emotionally broken to recognize how God continued to use us as His vessels. Broken vessels he remakes, dirty and sinful folk He makes clean, splintered and tortured souls Jesus can restore and reuse with a whole new purpose. As John 3:30 reminds us, He must increase and we must decrease…and Isaiah 61 says we are given a garment of praise to be called oaks of righteousness. God the Father had a plan and gave me a glimpse through a prophetic word that came to pass 5 years later after a season of brokenness and pain, showing me His strength and in my weakness He was made strong.

God continued to open doors after being 'left alone' but little did I know that God was re-forming me into what He saw rather than what I saw. A need in Haiti opened for teaching and translating for a medical team bringing supplies for a new clinic in the making and distributing food in two separate villages in the Cap Haitian area after the first earthquake. One of the engineers who had made several visits to Haiti reminded us as we distributed the food , 'don't forget to look them in the eyes as you give them these bags and boxes of food". I thought this a rather strange statement but then as I practiced what he suggested to us, I understood what loving my neighbor with a face and a smile was all about. Our LOVE for one another should not be indifferent or comfortable. It is more than writing a check or giving a gift card to someone in need. Our giving must cost us something to learn what Jesus lived. We might need to get ourselves in the grit of the situation to see what needs to be learned. This is yet another lesson in humility and Jesus' teaching us to walk equivocally in Grace and Truth. (John 1:14)

My ultimate lesson in surrender came when my husband's wedding ring was placed on the table of the restaurant. A 26-year marriage was ending and my life as I knew it was disintegrating. I was broken in body, soul, and heart. Two of my three girls were in college and the youngest was still in high school. It was a time when I had to LEAN like no other time in my life on the Lord. I had to learn on what I said I believed. I cried and retreated for a time as I could no longer function the same. What could I or should I do now? After crying out to the Lord, He told me to go to the mountain. I went on a retreat to the Trappist Abbey in the Shenandoah region of the Blue Ridge mountains and the

Lord was so gentle in speaking to me through the monks' vocal cantor of the Psalms. "Behold the Lamb of God who takes away the sins of the world," was the first truth brought to my spirit as a balm of healing. While reading Leviticus I was reminded about the 50th year of the fields and lying fallow in the year of Jubilee and the Israelites being set free. God showed me as I entered my 50th year of life on this earth that I was to remain with Him without being engaged in ANY ministry. It was a time to receive and learn and listen. It was my Jubilee of a new life of living and listening to the Father, Son and Holy Spirit. It was a challenge I had not encountered before, as I taught in a new school, moved into a new apartment, sold and parted with many of my possessions, battled serious depression, and had to begin again as God's beloved child.

During this Jubilee season, the Lord surrounded me with His people in my church at Opequon, my job with a collegial family and my three girls who were each reeling in their own pain, yet reached out to me in their own way at specific times that blessed me. God's promise in Hebrews 13:5-6 which states, I will never leave you nor forsake you, so we say with confidence, The Lord (Adonai) is my helper; and I will not be afraid...." These verses became my mantra as I walked on into what seemed like foggy nothingness for many days, weeks, and months. Finally, I realized through the opaque reality that God was filling me with His truth from His people and from His word, little by little. He put stalwarts of the faith in my path to sharpen me and challenge me as the proverb reminds us, "Iron sharpens iron," which gave me hope and direction in the midst of the tsunami of my life.

Throughout this new season of aloneness, Holy Spirit has been my steady force as I have learned beyond the dutiful, academic search of the divine to learn and grow through manifold means.

I prayed meditatively in His word and searched for those women who could mentor me and challenge me in my faith walk. I played the piano and sang hymns and worship songs to connect to Holy Spirit. I found a Lectio Divina group to learn new methods of prayer, then discovered Labyrinth prayer and the contemplative practice of Praying God's word and writing my prayers. Reading books like *One Thousand Gifts* by Ann Voskamp helped me to focus on gratitude and how to pinpoint five things each day to which I am grateful. Jesus truly has been my strength and song throughout this season of singleness and Divine discovery. There have been many challenges that range from financial to emotional, professional to spiritual all the while showing me sweet blessing and provision.

One last vignette is my pandemic surrender. In December 2019, I was reading *The Circle Maker* by Mark Batterson and setting some goals for the new year. I had gone on a little end of the year retreat (at the Trappist abbey) and heard the Lord impress upon me that some big changes were to come. I needed to let go of my "security" and trust Him completely. The things that gave me financial and professional security were my home and my job. In January 2020, I began to do a little research about the housing market and decided to put my house on the market in February 2020. I continued to trust the Lord but was still 'in the dark' as to where this was all going other than a potential move. I began to shed again the unnecessary things accumulated over the five years in my home. In March 2020, the real estate agent said the COVID 19 virus might affect the housing market, but not to worry. At the end of March, I had three potential buyers and agreements were made and my job as a teacher was "at home" by mid-March 2020 when I finished out the academic year. I was to move by the end of April or early May when the paperwork would be complete. My professional contract was not renewed due to moving too far to commute to that school. Thus by June 2020, I had let go of my home and job and now I truly was LEANING on God. God provided in a myriad of ways such as my daughter getting a full-time job in April 2020 and we moved in together to help one another. The sabbatical that I had been praying for years came to pass June-December 2020. Growing and being stretched in a new community and with a new way to grow with an online church became a lifeline for making authentic connections with people from around the country. God showed up and showed out as Pastor Mark Batterson loves to remind us and oh how grateful I am to be a part of His family, even in the midst of the COVID bubble.

Books that helped me grow in faith:

Love Does by Bob Goff
The Circle Maker by Mark Batterson
It's not Supposed to be this Way by Lysa Terkeurst
Resilience by Elizabeth Edwards
One Thousand Gifts by Ann Voskamp

JoEllen C. Delamatta

My name is JoEllen Cochran Delamatta and I was raised in the deep South on a pig farm, attended the same school for nine years, and then moved to the city of Hattiesburg for high school. Having attended the University of Southern Mississippi for four semesters, I transferred to Baylor University in Waco, Texas. This was the first time living outside of my family and my hometown and I was 20 years old. I graduated from Baylor University with a major in Religion and French and a minor in Psychology. After a year in Senegal, West Africa and getting married, I went to Trinity Divinity School in the Chicagoland area where I worked full time and studied part time for five years. I graduated with a Masters in Christian Thought with a focus in Theology and History and minor in Philosophy one week before my oldest daughter was born.

Becoming a Mother was such a welcome challenge and a blessing as I lived far from family during the infancy and younger years. Three daughters were born in the midst of five years as we prepared for Foreign ministry service and began work in West Africa.

After my studies, we lived in Senegal for two years as a family and later transferred to the Eastern suburbs of Paris, France where I worked for more than 13 years. I worked as a middle and high school Native English teacher, Drama teacher, and Exchange coordinator for European Campus Sainte Therese. During the academic breaks, I studied for my Masters of International Education through a satellite program in Kandern, Germany for three consecutive summers.

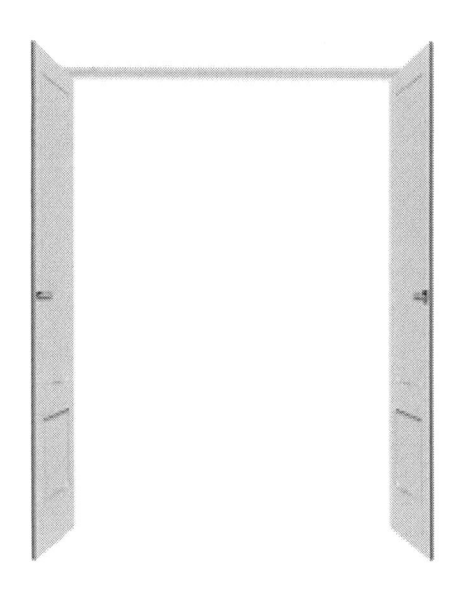

Moneshia R. Perkins
Yes, God!

How did you develop your faith when it seemed like nothing was going right in your life? Share a situation where you had to develop your faith walk.

It was hard to develop my faith in my lowest moments when things were not going right! I had to pray and cry out to God for forgiveness. You may ask why forgiveness? By asking God for forgiveness, I could have a clean slate with God in getting grounded in my situation. There was a relationship gone bad, business ties broken and being misunderstood in my family life. Three loved ones died in six months. I had to truly trust and lean on God with my whole heart, mind, and soul! I felt as though I was hanging on by a thread. I lost everything that I worked so hard for, only to be let down and violated by someone who was in my life for over three years.

As I analyzed what happened in my life and the decisions that I made during that time; I realized it was an illusion. God showed me every red flag and every lie that I did not see before. God gave me the courage and grace to correct my wrongs and admit to my misbehaving. Acknowledging my wrongs and asking for forgiveness helped me realize my fear of God. Confessing my sins and asking for clarity and atonement was important in my life! I had to cast my cares on God because he cares for me and loves me so much that he gave his life to me! Even though the enemy had me feeling that I was not worthy of forgiveness and that I would be damned for life; non-deserving of grace or forgiveness. God showed up and rendered the unrelenting grace and forgiveness I so desperately needed to move forward to heal!

In John 1:9 it states," When you confess your sins, God is faithful and just to forgive us of our sins and purify us from all unrighteousness". Henceforth, I grew stronger in the Lord by trusting him more and even redesigned my life with him by being baptized and studying his Word. I also learned to cast my cares on him because he truly cares for me. God has shown me how much he loves me by showing me how I was made in his own image! Even when I wanted to give up; I could not! There was this still sweet voice that kept telling me," You cannot give up NOW! Keep going! You will never know unless you finish!" God affirmed me and who I belonged to. God does not want our faith to falter. That is why he wants us in his Word daily to study to show ourselves approved unto God and his Word, keeping our strength in our daily journey.

In my process, I used wise and spiritual counselors to help me with other underlying issues that had stemmed from my childhood. In this process, I was also breaking generational curses that seemed to plaque our family for years. Having a prayer life of fasting and praying helps me get closer to God! It was an eye-opening experience to release things you love to gain something so much more than material things. The spiritual breakthroughs that you thought would not come to fruition. You know God is working! I kept my eye on the prize, and God showed me exactly what I needed for my journey. Gods' love superseded all our indiscretions! We are hard on ourselves, as it comes to forgiving ourselves and others.

God's grace and mercy is easy to get and so we must remember to give ourselves the same grace to grow stronger and believe Gods' power to take us beyond that barrier where the enemy tries to barricade us into the camp of indecisiveness and stagnation! I had to let go of my past, which was trying to keep me bound! I had to affirm my freedom daily until I broke the chains of the past in my spirit and my mind. Your mind is a battlefield, and you truly need the Word of God and prayer to battle to keep your mind! I found that fasting and being secluded was an integral part of my deliverance.

I had to relearn who I truly was in Christ and mean every word! I had to do the work. I had to do the exercises that were been assigned by my counselors. By golly it was not easy! By completing these life changing exercises, it showed me how I had lost myself in the process of manipulation. I could be free in my mind and in my thoughts, which was enlightening and uplifting. I felt liberated. My family and I mattered to God. It was such a relief to let go of things and the people who hurt me. I laid aside everything that would easily get me distracted. Grieving was a big part of my deliverance. I had trauma bonds that needed to be recognized and healed.

It was only God that kept me in this enduring process of being born again. "Lord whatever you do, please keep me close and please keep my Angels closer!" I love 2Corinthians 12:9, which states, "My Grace is sufficient for you!" God said," I knew you before you were conceived in the innermost parts of your mother's womb! I got you! I know your beginning, the in between and your end. Trust me, I will do something wonderful in your life. I do not know if anyone of you have dealt with low self-esteem, but I did. Depression, heartbreak and a loss in my business and it was challenge. However, God came in and showed me great and mighty acts of love! God turned my whole life around for the best! I am truly grateful and humbled that he came to save me, even in my mess. Glory be to God!

God did the extreme in my life! Out of the depths of my soul I cried out to God, and he showed up in my darkest hour of my life. This life-changing lesson has taught me to recognize that God wants to have a beautiful understanding relationship with me. He wants me to acknowledge that he is the author and finisher of my faith and my life. Our relationship is impeccable and peaceful. God has been that bridge over troubled waters and a wheel in the middle of a wheel on all levels of my life. God is my priest, protector, and provider. I could not have made it without him. God said, "That whatever seems dead, I will revive it and double it just for you!"

As I move forward in the most precious moments of my life, I can attest that," No weapon formed against me shall prosper and no tongue that shall rise against me in judgment thou shalt condemn". Isaiah 54:1.

I stand blessed and renewed day by day with an unwavering faith and trust in God that he can do anything but fail me. God can and will answer prayers and show you miracles that can change your life forever. Just knowing and believing that it could and would be done in his name. Hebrews 11:1 speaks volumes about how faith governs our lives when we really put it into action. We do not see a lot of things, but having the faith, asking God for intervention, believing and seeing it carried out in the spiritual realm is what God gets a kick out of daily. Through the process, God has renewed my mind daily, my heart, and my spirit. The process is not easy but a daily walk of life. I share my beautiful journey and space with those who appreciate my space and energy. I no longer try to conform to any negative energy that is not conducive to me. The best thing to do is release things and people who no longer serve you or who just tolerate you for what you can give them. Cut them off and get CPR for your soul from the Holy Spirit!

I learned to be content in my beautiful world. God has smiled on me and given me another chance to be great and live a wonder, peaceful and humble life. Everyday won't be peaches and crème, but I know that every that God has given me will be filled with joy, love, peace and grace. Give yourself grace today! You have come a long way when you bless your enemies and friends. My consolation in all of this is that God never sleeps or slumbers, but he will take care of you! The wicked will cease from trouble and their end will be as the grass withers and is thrown into the furnaces. Living in the present prevents me from living in the past; you cannot do both! Maintaining a mindset of living in faith; despite what you go through is a beast! You can be at war in your mind just to keep a steady stance in your situation. Your mind is a battlefield and as you tread in the marshes and overcome one situation at a time; God is building you to be stronger inside and out. Building spiritual muscle is part of being a believer.

We are not fighting against men, but spirits in high places. I had to put on the whole armor of God to stand in the evil day and, having done all to stand; I had to stand! Yes, I needed my helmet of salvation, breastplate of righteousness, sword of the Spirit, waist girded with truth, and feet shod with preparation of the gospel of peace. I knew what I had to do to get the results that I truly desired for my life! I gave others a chance or two instead of giving God that ultimate sacrifice in my life. Was it easy? Absolutely not! Doable and well worth it. That was the best decision in my life. If you are at the crossroads of life and you need a do over; try Jesus! He will make you over again and you will never be the same!

Trust him with your life and he will make all things new for you. Have the spirit of gratitude and speak your blessings to fruition. Trust and believe that he is, and he can and will do a perfect work in you! Forgive yourself and others now! Run to him in your spirit and he will shield you under his wings! God is faithful to his Word, and it will never come back void! I have never seen the righteous forsaken nor his seed begging bread. Try Jesus! God is love! Remember: Love is patient and love is kind. God will forever be with you, even until the end of time. Truly Goodness and Mercy shall follow you all the days of your life and you shall dwell in the house of the Lord forever!

Any last thoughts?

This life has many transitions, but with God, all things are possible. I am so glad that I gave my life to Christ! I am a Queen in Christ and you and I deserve the very best life offers all of us! Wherever you are in your life, just know that God is there with you. God is standing there waiting for you to ask for assistance. He loved us so much that he died on the cross for us! He knew everything about us before we were even born. I learned it is never too late to turn your life around. It is my prayer that God blesses you with a whole heart, mind, and spirit to live a peaceful and fruitful life. God has truly healed my mind, body and soul despite my transgressions. My faith is forever growing as well as my joy! I am grateful and humbled by this amazing life Christ has given me. Be blessed in the Lord and in the power of his might is my prayer.

Moneshia R. Perkins

I can truly say that God has truly been good to me. Through good and bad times, he never left me alone. I stand true to who I am in Christ. I am a virtuous Queen and mother of two beautiful daughters, Eneshia and Jaquese. I could have made it without their love and support. Life has thrown some curve balls, but God has always made it clear that with him all things are possible. I stand true to his Hold Word and his grace and mercy; I have the victory in him!

Life's experiences were lessons that needed to be taught to be a better person! I value these moments to embrace the success and grace that God has granted me as I live forward! Life is a most blessed gift!

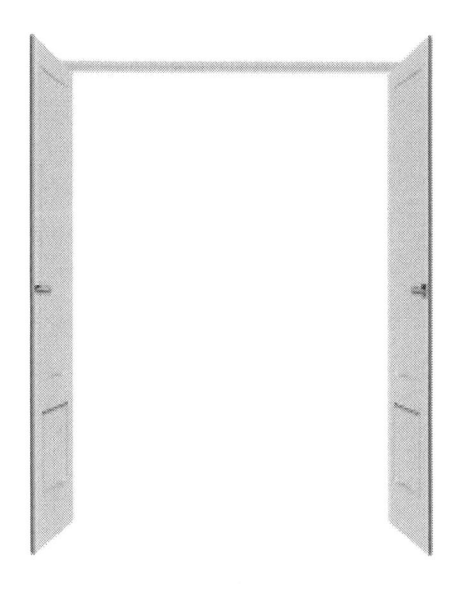

Cynthia Haymon
Yes, God!

My *yes God* moment. I had been married for two years. Everything was going great. I was in my last semester at Chicago State University working toward earning my BS in Criminal Justice. Everything was connecting the right way. Every major thing in my life was connected on the same major street in Chicago, Illinois. My mother's home where I grew up, my school, my children's school, the daycare my granddaughter attended my employer, which also was my place of worship. Between 95th and Throop Street to 95th and King Drive less than one mile. During that time, my life was comfortable and in order.

I loved working for the church, Trinity United Church of Christ, where Pastor Jeremiah A. Wright was the Senior Pastor. They employed me as one of many receptionists. With an awesome opportunity, being able to meet and greet all that came through the doors. This was my favorite job in the entire world. No other job made me feel complete as working in the house of the Lord. Every smiling face that came through those doors, each co-worker, every person who came for counseling or ministry or that came because of a death in their family, each person I embraced and enjoyed being there to serve them. I felt as if God Himself had smiled on me and that I was the apple of His eye.

No one could tell me otherwise. I loved working in the position that I held because I love working with God's people. Can you imagine the joy of working and worshipping in the same location? If we're experiencing a bad moment. I could go into the sanctuary or Wright Chapel and pray. I could meditate in many of the various rooms or go into the library and read during my lunch break, I could go to the credit union to make a deposit into my account or a withdraw, I could go to the Akiba Bookstore and purchase books, magazine or cd's or DVD's. The feeling of peace and joy was always there. I could feel God surrounding me there. I would leave there feeling as if I had no worries, not a care in the world.

God continued to bless me there. I meet and marry my second husband. He had been a deacon there for over twenty years. He and I both were active in several ministries within the church. This church had become a refuge for me. A place where God meets me at my lowest point and He gave me peace, he gave me love; He gave me hope, joy, understanding and wisdom and countless other blessings that are so many that I cannot list. One thing I know is that He was there for me.

After working within the church for several years, I received a job offer with a pay increase to work for the City of Chicago. I reluctantly accepted the position. This job doubled the increase in my income. I had never done the work that the position required, required however I figured I could do it. During this season in my life, various changes took place. Before taking this position, I was the Vice-President of the Board of Education for District #133, Riverdale, Illinois. Because I accepted the position with the city of Chicago, I was required to live within the city limits, so I moved to Chicago to fulfill those responsibilities. Removing myself from being an Elected Official within Riverdale School District was hard however, I knew that this decision was what God had for me. Yes, I would miss being there deciding for the schools. However, there was a newest of life that was awaiting me. There was the fear of the unknown, but God was with me, and the Holy Spirit was guiding me.

The last Sunday in August 2006 my husband had a heart attack while at church. He was rushed to Little Company of Mary Hospital in Evergreen Park, Illinois. He was a very healthy person. He only ate chicken and fish. He maintained a very healthy, nutritious diet. So, to hear that he had a heart attack was so alarming to us. He was discharged from the hospital several days later after a stent had been placed on his right leg. Everything seemed as if it were going back to normal, when in October he had another attack. However, this time he went to another hospital that was close to our home. During that hospital stay, we found out that he had a mass on his liver and was diagnosed with cancer of the liver.

Our entire world had changed. There were no signs. He had never been sick. Never seen in the hospital or even had any kind of illness. This diagnosis had taken us for a loop. All the scriptures that I had been reading and studying had to take the place of any doubt or disbelief that I was going to experience. Even if my husband couldn't, I had to stand by the promises of God. I had to trust God and trust the process. I had to understand that God's promises are yea and amen. Every word of God had to be the only words that I would stand on. I could not allow disbelief to be present within me. We had only been married less than two years.

February 7, 2007, my husband died at home while on hospice. From October 2006 until February 7, 2007, I trusted God and every word in the bible for healing every moment of the day for Don's healing. We prayed daily. I remember asking him if he believe God could heal him and he said, "people die with what I have." That statement hurt me to the core. However, it was what he believed. I watched him take his last breath. Have you ever since the life come out of a person? Their spirit man going back to the Creator. After it was over, the look of peace that comes just as if they were sleeping. Sitting there thinking well my best friend has gone, the only person who knew everything about me. I kept no secret from him.

Our friendship was just so amazing. However, now that friendship no longer exists. What now? How do I go on? Lord, what's next? Who can I confide in? Who can I tell when I am thinking thoughts that are ungodly? Who is going to laugh with me in the middle of the night? Who is going to hold me when I will vulnerable? Who is going to comfort me when uncertain things happen? Who can I tell my fears and insecurities?

Later I felt that I was cheated from spending years with him. He transitioned two days after our second-year anniversary. His death was on my brother's birthday, and I had to have his funeral on my sister's birthday five days later so that his only surviving sister could attend, who had just lost her daughter to cancer a few months earlier and she was going into the hospital to have a procedure because she had cancer. It was the wisdom of one of our friend's that I shared my anger with about the time we had together. As I was complaining, this friend said that "it is not the quantity of time but the quality of time." At that moment, I could no longer act out with God because He called His son home. That Don belonged to God and not to me. That God allowed us to feel that love that can only come from Him, I understood we had a beautiful marriage even if it was not long. We had a love for each other that God gave us. After his death, there was a feeling of loneliness that I had never felt before. There was an emptiness in my soul. I fell into a depression, and I got sick. I was diagnosed with type II diabetes three months after Don passed away. Even with this illness, I could not shake the depression and losing my husband. I went into a lonely place that only God could bring me out of. I was not happy. It seemed as if I was just existing and not living.

Death was trying to take a hold of me. The enemy had his eye on me to take me out. Because he knew what God had in store for me. As I remember that during the transitioning of Don, I went to church one evening just to be in the presence of God. It was a Thursday, and that was the day that the sanctuary choir rehearsal. As I sat in the sanctuary, a friend of ours saw me and he was telling me about bible study class that night that had been in the book Job. I knew that word he was given me was for Don. However, that word was to let me know what I was getting ready to endure.

Job 1:6 12 KJV *6 Now there was a day when the sons of God came to present themselves before the LORD, and [e]Satan also came among them. 7 And the LORD said to [f]Satan, "From where do you come?" So Satan answered the LORD and said, "From going to and fro on the earth, and from walking back and forth on it." 8 Then the LORD said to Satan, "Have you [g]considered My servant Job, that there is none like him on the earth, a blameless and upright man, one who fears God and [h]shuns evil?" 9 So Satan answered the LORD and said, "Does Job fear God for nothing? 10 Have You not [i]made a hedge around him, around his household, and around all that he has on every side? You have blessed the work of his hands, and his possessions have increased in the land. 11 But now, stretch out Your hand and touch all that he has, and he will surely curse[j] You to Your face!" 12 And the LORD said to Satan, "Behold, all that he has is in* *your [k]power; only do not lay a hand on his person." So, Satan went out from the presence of the LORD.*

Just as Job went through various situations and circumstances, I too also went through. I lost a husband; I got sick; I lost a job and just about everything that I had was lost. I could not understand what was going on and why I was under attack. Until the Holy Spirit reminded me of the conversation that I had with our friend. It was at that moment I knew God was directing and ordering my steps even though it was not comfortable. The Holy Spirit had prepared me for what I was getting ready to endure. Even to the point of showing a reference in His Word. I understood He could allow the enemy to take things away from me, but he could not take my life. He had no authority to take my life, because my life belonged to a powerful Almighty God that promised never to leave me nor forsake me. The realization of this my thoughts became under submission of the Holy Spirit. I had a connection that was unbreakable; I had a God that keep me though the storms kept raging in my life. My soul has been anchored in the Lord.

God placed a praise so deep within me and He gave me the strength to lift my hands in total praise unto Him. So, I began to be like the scripture **Philippians 2:5 KJV**, *"Let this mind be in you that is also in Christ Jesus."*

Coming out of this dark place, I had to seek the Lord. Isaiah 55:6-7 KJV

Seek ye the LORD while he may be found, call ye upon him while he is near: let the wicked forsake his way, and the unrighteous man his thoughts: and let him return unto the

LORD, and he will have mercy upon him; and to our God, for he will abundantly pardon.

I rested again on the promises of God. I meditated on the Word to bring me up out of the mindset that I had been in. Determined not to allow the enemy to have victory, I got busy applying the promises of God to every situation that had been presented to me. I knew I believed God's Word, I knew it was only be His Word that deliverance would come. I knew the same way I felt God could heal and deliver Don. He could do it for me. I knew I had to bring God in remembrance of His word.

There were so many scriptures I used to bring me out such as:

"**2 Corinthians 10:4-5 KJV** - *4* For the weapons of our warfare *are* not [a]carnal but mighty in God for pulling down strongholds, *5* casting down arguments and every high thing that exalts itself against the knowledge of God, bringing every thought into captivity to the obedience of Christ.

Hebrews 11:1 KJV *Now Faith is the substance of things hoped for the evidence of things not seen.*

Psalms 91:1 KJV *He who dwells in the secret place of the Most High Shall abide under the shadow of the Almighty. 2 I will say of the LORD, "He is my refuge and my fortress; My God, in Him I will trust.*

Psalm 118:17 KJV *17 I shall not die, but live, and declare the works of the LORD.*

Isaiah 53:4-5 KJV *4 Surely He has borne our [g]griefs And carried our [h]sorrows; Yet we [i]esteemed Him stricken,*

[i]*Smitten by God, and afflicted.* *⁵ But He was wounded*[k] *for our transgressions, He was* [l]*bruised for our iniquities; The chastisement for our peace was upon Him, And by His stripes*[m] *we are healed.*

Psalm 51:1 KJV *Have mercy upon me, O God, According to Your lovingkindness; According to the multitude of Your tender mercies, Blot out my transgressions.*

Psalm27:1 KJV *The LORD is my light and my salvation; Whom shall I fear? The LORD is the strength of my life; Of whom shall I be afraid?*

Psalm 34: 1-3 KJV *I will bless the LORD at all times; His praise shall continually be in my mouth.* *² My soul shall make its boast in the LORD; The humble shall hear of it and be glad.* *³ Oh, magnify the LORD with me, And let us exalt His name together."*

Psalm 100 KJV *Make a joyful shout to the LORD,* [a]*all you lands!* *² Serve the LORD with gladness; Come before His presence with singing.* *³ Know that the LORD, He is God; It is He who has made us, and* [b]*not we ourselves; We are His people and the sheep of His pasture.* *⁴ Enter into His gates with thanksgiving, And into His courts with praise. e thankful to Him, and bless His name.* *⁵ For the LORD is good; His mercy is everlasting, And His truth endures to all generations.*

Psalm 46 *"God is our refuge and strength, a very present help in trouble.* *² Therefore will not we fear, though the earth be removed, and though the mountains be carried into the midst of the sea;* *³ Though the waters thereof roar and be troubled, though the mountains shake with the swelling thereof. Selah.* *⁴ There is a river, the streams whereof shall make glad the city of God, the holy place of the tabernacles* *of the most High.* *⁵ God is in the midst of her; she shall not be moved: God shall help her, and that right early. ⁶ The heathen raged, the kingdoms were moved: he uttered his voice, the earth melted. ⁷ The* LORD *of hosts is with us; the God of Jacob is our refuge. Selah. ⁸ Come, behold the works of the* LORD*, what desolations he hath made in the earth. ⁹ He maketh wars to cease unto the end of the earth; he breaketh the bow, and cutteth the spear in sunder; he burneth the chariot in the fire. ¹⁰ Be still, and know that I am God: I will be exalted among the heathen, I will be exalted in the earth. ¹¹ The* LORD *of hosts is with us; the God of Jacob is our refuge. Selah.*

I search for every scripture with healing, every scripture with joy, peace, praise, and prayer. I took every scripture back to God. Because God said in **Isaiah 43:26 KJV** *²⁶ Put Me in remembrance; Let us contend together; State your case, that you may be [a]acquitted.* If you are reading this, God has this set out just for you.

There are so many scriptures in God's Word that has your name on it. There is no situation that He cannot handle. The angels reminded Sarah by asking her in **Genesis 18:14 KJV** *¹⁴ Is any thing too hard for the* LORD*?*

When the cares of life weigh you down, get into His word for the strength and peace you will need. Study the Word of God so that your spirit can be quicken when the enemy will attack. It is a guarantee that you will come under attack, and it is a guarantee that with the Word in you, your attack won't overwhelm you. Praise God in season and out of season. When things are good and when things are bad. Worship Him when you feel like it and when you don't. Because that is how Him will carry you through. Remember that King David was a worshipper, he was the "apple of God's eye."

Yet even David had a cross to bear. Jesus paid the price for our cross however, we still must go through the storm.

But we win, because the battle is not yours. It's the Lord's.

Pastor Elect Cynthia Haymon

Rev. Cynthia Haymon is the Pastor Elect of Resurrection House Baptist Church of Northwest Indiana. Located in Gary, Indiana. Sharing in ministry with her husband Overseer Rev. Dr. Mozell Haymon they were planted from RHBC Dolton, Illinois under the leadership of Bishop Marcus Allen Randle and Rev Mattie L Randle. She has been in ministry for over ten years ministering the Word of the Lord. She holds a BS in Criminal Justice from Chicago State University, MPA in Public Administration from Keller Graduate School of Management and in pursuit of a MDiv from Midwestern Baptist Theological Seminary in Kansas, Missouri.

She is a business owner of CGM Consultants, Inc and CGM Cleaning and Janitorial Services. She is the former Vice-President of School District #133, Riverdale Illinois. Member of WOW – Women Organizing Women, Founder of WOFFC – Women On Fire For Christ, member of Criminal Justice Association, board member of Serenity House of Gary, Indiana, case manager for Sojourner Truth House of Gary, Indiana. 2009 Award Recipient Black Essence Award for Community and Ministry.

Together Cynthia and Mozell Haymon share ten children, 15 grandchildren and 6 great grandchildren. Understanding that marriage is ministry within itself. "God has truly blessed our union with his gift of love, joy, peace and sometimes long suffering. But through it all it is an honor to work together daily in the work of the Lord. Powerful pillars in the community. With the understanding that "to whom much is given, much is required."

Gloria Berry
Yes, God!

When I received the invitation to take part in being an author for this book, the instructions were to share a bible verse that relates to my journey with God. We were also asked to describe when I said yes to God. I decided the best bible verse for me comes from the book of Psalms chapter 84:11-13. "For the Lord God is a sun and shield the Lord will give grace and glory no good thing will he withhold from them that walk, uprightly oh Lord of hosts blessed is the man that trusted in thee."

I had a decent life. I have had difficulties, but mostly I can't complain. What good would complaining do anyway, right? My life wasn't that bad, and I believe it got comfortable. I maneuvered through racism, and sexism and although my childhood was difficult, I know it was much better than a lot of others. Fast forward to 2012. You could say that I found myself when the rug was pulled out from under me. I remember shortly before my world fell apart; I was in a community theater play. While I was on break during the play backstage, one of the young actors was talking about Jesus, the bible, and how much religion is The White Man's religion. I'll never forget to tell him I know what you mean. Jesus is not the god that has been taught to us. I've always regretted saying that.

Fast forward to February 12, 2012. I found myself to be sickly. The first signs started showing in 2009, but by 2012, I was near death. My red blood cell count was very low. I had a mysterious rash. Then I went from a size 14 to a zero. I developed chest pains and fatigue. I went to the hospital, and I was told I had severe asthma and was given an inhaler. Mostly doctors could not figure out what was wrong with me. Another major symptom was severe insomnia. I could stay up for 72 hours before I could fall asleep out of fatigue. I also was told at a community free medical event at the Oakland Coliseum that my ribs were misaligned. They even adjusted my ribs, and it took the pain off my lungs, which gave me some relief. So, I thought they solved part of the problem. I also went to a free clinic near my house, and they didn't understand what was wrong with me. They suggested I had allergies, and then prescribed me Ambien to help with my insomnia. My first dose of Ambien was 5 mg. The 5 mg got me to sleep, but not throughout the night. The doctor then increased my dose to 10 mg. Once I started taking 10 mg of Ambien, I found out quickly how dangerous and careful you must be with this powerful drug.

    This happened. I took my Ambien to go to sleep, and at the time I did not understand that you could think while you were awake, but you were sleepwalking. I had a friend in prison that I visited a few times. After taking Ambien one night, I went to visit my friend in prison who was four hours away. My thought was how tired I was from visiting my friend and that I wanted to tell him to his face that I would no longer be making the trip. I drove on Ambien down to the prison and walked through the visiting room processing area. I completed the process that I knew very well and walked through the metal detector to go into the visiting room. After I walked through the metal detector, the guard told me I could not proceed with my visit because I smelled like weed. I let the guard know that I smelled like weed because I had been around some. The next thing I knew, other guards approached me and asked me to step into the Sergeant's office. They then handcuffed me and patted me down. They told me I smelled like weed. I had the smell of weed in my clothes, and I knew from my experience in visiting that there is a visiting center that has clothes that people can change into. I then asked the guards if I could change my clothes because they smelled like weed.

The guards refused my suggestion and took me to another bigger room. The guards kept saying I was bringing marijuana into the visiting room. I kept insisting that I wasn't, but I thought eventually these people would let me go. Hours went by. They kept giving me water, and I had to use the restroom very badly. I had very severe gastroenterology problems which was another symptom of my illness, and I needed to go to the restroom. They sent me to the restroom with two female officers. One officer put a trash bag on the toilet. Handcuffed, I was instructed to use the restroom. I used the restroom and was not given anything to wipe myself. I was then told to stand in the corner and bend over, and the officers visually checked me and what was in the toilet.

One officer took me back to the other visiting room while the other officer gathered the trash bag of feces. The officer that carried the bag dropped it and officers just kept telling me I was bringing marijuana into the prison. The officer who searched the feces that she dropped let the other officers know that there was nothing to be found, but they kept interrogating me. I had to use the restroom again, and the same thing happened. minus the dropping of the feces. Next, I was told that there was going to be a search warrant. At this point, I already did not trust these officers, but I did not feel comfortable about them presenting a search warrant. One of the officers did not talk to me rudely and answered my questions, so I asked her how I would know if the search warrant was valid. This officer stated that there would be a wet signature from the judge and a number on it. So quickly after that, a search warrant appeared, the search warrant did not look official to me at all. It looked like a template, and I had a problem believing that the judge would sign something like that, and how it was accomplished on a Saturday. The officers told me that I needed to take all my clothes off. I felt that that would be too embarrassing, they had already strip-searched me in the bathroom, and I believed that any minute they were going to release me. After about five hours, my wrists hurt very badly from the handcuffs, and I begged the officers to take them off. Eventually, they took the handcuffs off and asked me again to remove all my clothes, and I refused. After this last request from the officers for me to move my clothes, they stood up, put handcuffs on me, and told me I was being arrested for contempt of court. That did not make sense to me at all. One, we were not in a courtroom, and I had the right to refuse a search although if the warrant were valid they could search me by force. So, after they told me I was arrested they said we need to pat you down for safety. I thought that was strange because I had already been patted down twice and strip-searched twice so what could they feel I could have? One officer asked me if I had anything that could hurt them from patting me down and again I thought that was strange because they had already patted me down. They did not strip-search me. When they went to pat me down they went right into my coat pocket and took the keys to my car. They then sat me down and went outside and searched for my car. They then brought everything they found from my car into the visiting room. This included some marijuana. They then took me to the county jail and booked me for nine felonies. When I got my booking report, the first thing that stood out to me was a charge for gang activity. I asked the clerk at the jail why that charge was on there. She then talked to the officers and gave me a new booking sheet. The new booking sheet said that count one, the game activity charge, was entered in error. The officers then took me to the strip-out area, and I knew at that point that I would have to remove all my clothes, or they would remove them for me. I cannot explain how dehumanizing it was to remove all my clothes, turn around, bend over, spread my buttocks, and cough. The officers who brought me from the prison asked the search officer what they found, and the search officer said nothing. I thought I would be released, but the fact that my car was parked in their parking lot, regardless of the I did not have anything on me behind the prison walls, made it a felony. So, they put me in my jail cell. I cried my eyes out, and then got on my knees. I said if Jesus is real, please release me tomorrow. Seven days later I was still in jail, until my family and friends bailed me out.

For the next two years, I went to court, criminal and civil, forty-seven times. As the months went by after I was arrested my health worsened. By June 2012, a doctor called me on a Saturday and gave me a direct order to go to the emergency room for a blood transfusion. I did not know that doctors even gave these types of orders. I was near death. I was not very aware of what was going on. I had mixed feelings about blood transfusions. I truly don't even remember receiving it. I was so weak and had adapted to being so unhealthy. The hospital ended up keeping me for 12 to 14 days. I'm not sure how long I was there. They tried all kinds of tests on me to try to diagnose what was wrong with me. I had endoscopies, colonoscopies, a sore cut out my back with a biopsy on that, CAT scan, MRIs, EKGs, and the most horrific of all a bone marrow test. For the bone marrow test, they took a corkscrew-like tool and inserted it into my hip bone. I had a few Vicodin for pain before this, so I snuck and took a Vicodin. Then before they did the procedure I asked them if they were going to give me anything for pain from the procedure and they gave me a Vicodin. When they put that tool through my bone, the pain was more excruciating than having a baby. The Vicodin was not effective. My mother and daughter were there. My mother could not take it and ended up leaving the room, my brave daughter stayed near me. Later my mother told me she could hear me screaming from outside. A cancer doctor ended up taking over my case, and diagnosed me, with **Hypereosinophilia**. It's a rare blood disease that's very hard to explain to people, even Doctors. I was prescribed a very high dose of steroids, which helped me get stronger, and kill the white blood cells that were in abundance.. I slowly start feeling stronger, but the rage associated with the high dose of steroids is real. Also, I could physically feel my bones getting stronger in 4 months depending on the dose. I could always feel my bones either getting stronger or weaker and it was very painful. During this time frame, I was too weak to work and lost my house. My daughter and I had nowhere to go. I was facing prison time, and I moved in with my sister. My daughter moved in with my mom and sometimes with her boyfriend. It was very painful to not be able to provide for my daughter. It was also painful to know that I would not be leaving my daughter any property if I should leave this earth. I ended up not being able to stay with my sister after some months because of my dog. I then became a caretaker, ironically of someone who was in prison when I worked at one six years prior. but because of my dog, I lost that place too. I then ended up renting out someone's garage that was converted into a studio, but each month I struggled to pay my rent, because of my low energy and inability to work consistently. Ironically, the lady who rented the place to me often displayed a dislike for me, but I will never forget what she once said to me. She said, "Gloria, I don't know why you are going through all the things you are going through but when you get through this storm your blessings are going to rain down on you." She said it with such conviction, that I believed her. So, I moved into a shelter. The shelter would not take me because I had a job, and they said they only had two beds for Women that work and they were filled. The next day I lied to the shelter and told them I did not work, and they said I'd have to show proof that I was on welfare which I could not, so I ended up sleeping on my mother's couch.

These two years were the roughest time of my life. I ended up getting off the steroids and on chemotherapy, which was very frightening for me. Every time I had to make a court appearance I feared I'd be taken into custody. I ended up hiring a lawyer who knew I was overcharged for the case and got different charges dismissed. I was desperate and knew I needed spiritual guidance to get through it. I started attending Church more, and due to a friend constantly telling me I should attend Glide Bible study in San Francisco, I decided to give it a try. Every Bible study I would cry. The group would pray very hard for me and lay hands on me. I felt like I had a spiritual family and consistently went every Tuesday night. The Bible study was led by Pastor Harry Williams. I love him to this day. He would always ask for prayer requests and pray for everyone. He'd also have a check-in time. There was one brother named Ricky who would always say he was grateful. His saying has always stuck with me, and I challenged myself to seek to be grateful regardless of my circumstances. Bible study gave me many tools to be stronger. Like at court appearances when I wanted to cry I would just look at the judge like he was Goliath, and I was David. It gave me so much strength. When it got closer to my trial date, I had faith that they would be done.

I ended up being found guilty and sentenced to six months in county jail. I went to jail with my head held high and focused on working on trying to get out earlier, reading the Bible from beginning to end, writing a book, and developing my plan to start a girls' group. Every evening, I asked my cellmate to say something for which she was thankful. When I thought she was tired of me doing it I stopped, and she told me she wanted me to continue doing it. I went to the jail Bible study, but I didn't like it because the Chaplain was putting us down. I started my own Bible study and ended up with twelve Women at one point attending. It became such a beautiful thing. I mimicked the way Pastor Williams conducted his Bible study. My cellmate told me she never believed in God but because of me she does. I had girls running up to me to share what blessings they received throughout my months incarcerated.. While in jail I said yes to God and believed with all my heart once I made it through this rough time in my life my blessings would flow. I began to get excited about my future.

When I was released I had a blessing right away. I was released at one in the morning and could not see in front of me because of the fog and didn't know which way to go. Another Woman got released and offered me a ride to Walmart to buy some clothes that fit me, I gained fifty pounds. She also gave me a ride to a hotel a Pastor I knew had bought for me. When I got to the hotel, I was only booked for one night and needed two. The clerk blessed me with a free night. When I got back home I went into transitional housing. They never had safe places to offer me to live in then after nine months I got a call that there was an apartment. I also got approved for a Veterans housing voucher. I viewed the apartment that I was told about with around fifteen other people. I said to God thy will be done and they picked me for the apartment. I was so thankful I was thanking God for drawers in the kitchen, ha-ha. I then went to a Veteran program, and they got me approved for Veterans' Compensation.

Once stable I became an activist in the community. I ran for District Supervisor and received over 4,000 votes with only a $900 budget. I did not win but kept getting involved. I ran for State delegate and was the only progressive candidate in San Francisco to win. I won by five votes. I then ran for San Francisco Democratic Central Committee and was the only candidate not supported by the establishment to win with over 26,000 votes. Since this I have been on the Guaranteed Income Committee, presently on the Reparations committee, started my girls' organization and last year opened a business. I have an alarm on my phone at 5 pm every day to make sure I thank God for what I am thankful. I went through what I went through not because I deserved it but so that I can tell somebody and most of all give all Glory to God. Now when I speak on homelessness, the criminal justice system, and what can happen when you have faith, I have a story that might encourage someone on their journey to say Yes to God. Amen.

40 Christian Inspirational Quotes

1. "Life is wasted if we do not grasp the glory of the cross, cherish it for the treasure that it is, and cleave to it as the highest price of every pleasure and the deepest comfort in every pain. What was once foolishness to us—a crucified God—must become our wisdom and our power and our only boast in this world." - **John Piper**

2. "God loves each of us as if there were only one of us" - **Augustine**

3. "God never said that the journey would be easy, but He did say that the arrival would be worthwhile" - **Max Lucado**

4. "God's work done in God's way will never lack God's supplies." - **Hudson Taylor**

5. "God will meet you where you are in order to take you where He wants you to go." - **Tony Evans**

6. "Let God's promises shine on your problems." - **Corrie ten Boom**

7. "Christ literally walked in our shoes." - **Tim Keller**

8. "He is no fool who gives what he cannot keep, to gain what he cannot lose." - **Jim Elliot**

9. "Remember who you are. Don't compromise for anyone, for any reason. You are a child of the Almighty God. Live that truth." - **Lysa Terkeurst**

10. "If you can't fly, then run, If you can't run, then walk, If you can't walk, then crawl, but whatever you do, you have to keep moving forward." - **Martin Luther King Jr.**

11. "Our greatest fear should not be of failure but of succeeding at things in life that don't really matter."
- **Francis Chan**

12. "If God is your partner, make your plans BIG!" – **D.L. Moody**

13. "You are the only Bible some unbelievers will ever read." - **John MacArthur**

14. "We gain strength, and courage, and confidence by each experience in which we really stop to look fear in the face...we must do that which we think we cannot." - **Eleanor Roosevelt**

15. "He who lays up treasures on earth spends his life backing away from his treasures. To him, death is loss. He who lays up treasures in heaven looks forward to eternity; he's moving daily toward his treasures. To him, death is gain." - **Randy Alcorn**

16. "God does not give us everything we want, but He does fulfill His promises, leading us along the best and straightest paths to Himself." - **Dietrich Bonhoeffer**

17. "The Christian life is not a constant high. I have my moments of deep discouragement. I have to go to God in prayer with tears in my eyes, and say, 'O God, forgive me,' or 'Help me.'" - **Billy Graham**

18. "Always, everywhere God is present, and always He seeks to discover Himself to each one" - **A.W. Tozer**

19. "If you believe in a God who controls the big things, you have to believe in a God who controls the little things. It is we, of course, to whom things look 'little' or 'big'." - **Elisabeth Elliot**

20. "There is no one who is insignificant in the purpose of God." - **Alistair Begg**

21. "Relying on God has to start all over everyday, as if nothing has yet been done." –**C. S. Lewis**

22. "This is our time on the history line of God. This is it. What will we do with the one deep exhale of God on this earth? For we are but a vapor and we have to make it count. We're on. Direct us, Lord, and get us on our feet."
- **Beth Moore**

23. "The best thing about the future is that it comes only one day at a time." - **Abraham Lincoln**

24. "Your potential is the sum of all the possibilities God has for your life." - **Charles Stanley**

25. "The best and most beautiful things in this world cannot be seen or even heard, but must be felt with the heart."
- **Helen Keller**

26. "We are all faced with a series of great opportunities brilliantly disguised as impossible situations."
- **Chuck Swindoll**

27. "Be faithful in small things because it is in them that your strength lies." - **Mother Teresa**

28. "The greater your knowledge of the goodness and grace of God on your life, the more likely you are to praise Him in the storm." - **Matt Chandler**

29. "Continuous effort -- not strength nor intelligence -- is the key to unlocking our potential." - **Winston Churchill**

30. "God is most glorified in us when we are most satisfied in Him" - **John Piper**

31. "Faith does not eliminate questions. But faith knows where to take them." - **Elisabeth Elliot**

32. "God will meet you where you are in order to take you where He wants you to go." - **Tony Evans**

33. "Worry does not empty tomorrow of its sorrows; it empties today of its strength." - **Corrie Ten Boom**

34. "The will of God will not take us where the grace of God cannot sustain us." - **Billy Graham**

35. "The greater your knowledge of the goodness and grace of God on your life, the more likely you are to praise Him in the storm." - **Matt Chandler**

36. "God is able to take the mess of our past and turn it into a message. He takes the trials and tests and turns them into a testimony." - **Christine Caine**

37. "What gives me the most hope every day is God's grace; knowing that his grace is going to give me the strength for whatever I face, knowing that nothing is a surprise to God." - **Rick Warren**

38. "Remember Whose you are and Whom you serve. Provoke yourself by recollection, and your affection for God will increase tenfold; your imagination will not be starved any longer, but will be quick and enthusiastic, and your hope will be inexpressibly bright."
-Oswald Chambers

39. "We can see hope in the midst of hopelessness. We can see peace in the midst of chaos. We have a hope that the world does not have. We can see clearly that all things work together for the good of them that love Him and are called according to His purpose." **- Priscilla Shirer**

40. "There is not a single thing that Jesus cannot change, control, and conquer because he is the living Lord."
- Franklin Graham

50 Comforting Bible Verses That Will Envelop You Like a Warm Blanket

In troubled times during loss, sadness, or sickness, look to these encouraging psalms.

When searching for comfort in times of stress or loss, it can be easy to lean into the things that make us feel the most relaxed — maybe a favorite television show, a long walk outside, or reading a good book. But for people of faith, finding comfort can be something much more spiritual. Reciting Bible verses for anxiety or thinking about inspirational women in the Bible, even, can be something that brings peace and calm during chaos. Sometimes, though, you need as much support as you can get from scripture.

That's why having a running list of comforting Bible verses is such an important tool for a Christian to have access to. They can provide some solace after a loved one's death or be the encouraging words of hope you need. You can read one daily when you need motivation to face the world or recite them to a friend who has fallen on hard times. No matter how you choose to incorporate comforting psalms in your everyday life, just knowing that you can quickly find verses that bring you peace, calm, and perspective is more important than you might think. If you're looking for an easy-to-access list of comforting Bible verses, here are some to choose from.

John 1:9

"If we confess our sins, he is faithful and just and will forgive us our sins and purify us from all unrighteousness."

- **The Good News:** Every person makes mistakes. No one is perfect. But owning up to those mistakes can clear the slate.

Deuteronomy 31:8

"The Lord himself goes before you and will be with you; he will never leave you nor forsake you. Do not be afraid; not not be discouraged."

- **The Good News:** Trust that the lord will guide you out of any difficult situation.

John 16:22

"So with you: Now is your time of grief, but I will see you again and you will rejoice, and no one will take away your joy."

- **The Good News:** You are the only person who can control your joy — don't give that power to anyone else.

Romans 15:13

"May the God of hope fill you with all joy and peace as you trust in him, so that you may overflow with hope by the power of the Holy Spirit."

- **The Good News:** If you allow it, the Holy Spirit can provide strength when you are lacking it.

Psalm 46:1

"God is our refuge and strength, an ever-present help in trouble."

- **The Good News:** God will always help you through, regardless of your relationship with him.

Psalm 23:4

"Even though I walk through the valley of the shadow of death, I will fear no evil, for you are with me; your rod and your staff, they comfort me."

- **The Good News:** Even death cannot separate us from the never-failing love of God.

Romans 8:35, 37

"Who shall separate us from the love of Christ? Shall tribulation, or distress, or persecution, or famine, or nakedness, or danger, or sword? No, in all these things we are more than conquerors through him who loved us."

- **The Good News:** God gives us the power to overcome any circumstance, no matter how daunting or overwhelming.

Deuteronomy 7:9

"Know therefore that the Lord your God is God, the faithful God who keeps covenant and steadfast love with those who love him and keep his commandments, to a thousand generations."

The Good News: Over and over, the Bible affirms God's love as "steadfast." In other words, it is available to those who need it, whenever they need it.

Psalm 119:49–50

"Remember your word to your servant, in which you have made me hope. This is my comfort in my affliction, that your promise gives me life."

- **The Good News:** Don't lose hope. God's promises never falter.

Isaiah 40: 28, 31

"They who wait for the Lord shall renew their strength; they shall mount up with wings like eagles, they shall run and not be weary; they shall walk and not faint."

- **The Good News:** Those who call on the Lord in faith will find strength they did not know they possessed.

John 3:16–17

"For God so loved the world, that he gave his only Son, that whoever believes in him should not perish but have eternal life. For God did not send his Son into the world to condemn the world, but in order that the world might be saved through him."

- **The Good News:** Salvation (as well as the confidence that comes with it) is always available to us through the grace of Jesus Christ.

Isaiah 49:13

"Sing for joy, O heavens, and exult, O earth; break forth, O mountains, into singing! For the Lord has comforted his people and will have compassion on his afflicted."

- **The Good News:** There is no suffering beyond the reach of our merciful God.

Matthew 5:3–5

"Blessed are the poor in spirit, for theirs is the kingdom of heaven. Blessed are those who mourn, for they shall be comforted. Blessed are the meek, for they shall inherit the earth."

- **The Good News:** God's love and mercy transcend and confound the expectations of this world.

Isaiah 51:12

"I, I am he who comforts you; who are you that you are afraid of man who dies, of the son of man who is made like grass."

- **The Good News:** Don't be afraid of anyone; your enemies will wither away. God is forever.

Romans 5:1–2

"Therefore, since we have been justified by faith, we have peace with God through our Lord Jesus Christ. Through him we have also obtained access by faith into this grace in which we stand, and we rejoice in hope of the glory of God."

- **The Good News:** We stand firm in our faith and in the gift of grace freely granted us through Jesus Christ our Lord.

Lamentations 3:22–23

"The steadfast love of the Lord never ceases, his mercies never come to an end; they are new every morning; great is your faithfulness."

- **The Good News:** God's comfort is renewed over and over again.

Isaiah 66:13

"As one whom his mother comforts, so I will comfort you; you shall be comforted in Jerusalem."

- **The Good News:** God's love will tenderly nurture you as a mother nurtures a child.

Romans 8:28

"And we know that for those who love God all things work together for good, for those who are called according to his purpose."

- **The Good News:** God wills nothing but good for us.

Psalm 31:7

"I will rejoice and be glad in your steadfast love, because you have seen my affliction; you have known the distress of my soul."

- **The Good News:** God knows your suffering, God feels your pain, God knows you better than you know yourself.

Romans 8:38–39

"For I am sure that neither death nor life, nor angels nor rulers, nor things present nor things to come, nor powers, nor height nor depth, nor anything else in all creation, will be able to separate us from the love of God in Christ Jesus our Lord."

- **The Good News:** There is nothing on the face of the earth, not even death itself, that is powerful enough to separate us from the love of God.

Psalm 27:12

"Deliver me not unto the will of mine enemies: for false witnesses are risen up against me, and such as breathe out cruelty."

- **The Good News:** God will offer protection and comfort to you, no matter how many enemies you have.

Isaiah 41:10

"So do not fear, for I am with you; do not be dismayed, for I am your God. I will strengthen you and help you; I will uphold my righteous right hand."

- **The Good News:** God is always with you, giving you strength whenever you may need it.

John 16:22

"So with you: Now is your time of grief, but I will see you again and you will rejoice, and no one will take away your joy."

- **The Good News:** Grief comes and goes, but joy will come, and God will be there throughout every high and low.

Psalm 116:1-2

"I love the Lord, for he heard my voice; he heard my cry for mercy. Because he turned his ear to me, I will call on him as long as I live."

- **The Good News:** When you cry out for God, he hears you, no matter how long it's been since you last prayed or cried out for him.

Deuteronomy 31:6

"Be strong and courageous. Do not be afraid or terrified because of them, for the Lord your God goes with you; he will never leave you nor forsake you."

- **The Good News:** Wherever you go, God is there, so there is no reason to be afraid.

Romans 8:24

"For in this hope we were saved. But hope that is seen is no hope at all. Who hopes for what they already have?"

- **The Good News:** God is the ultimate source of hope.

Psalm 31:24

"Be strong and take heart, all you who hope in the Lord."

- **The Good News:** If you have the Lord, then you have strength.

2 Corinthians 4:16-18

"Therefore we do not lose heart. Though outwardly we are wasting away, yet inwardly we are being renewed day by day. For our light and momentary troubles are achieving for us an eternal glory that far outweighs them all. So we fix our eyes not on what is seen, but on what is unseen, since what is seen is temporary, but what is unseen is eternal."

- **The Good News:** Every bit of momentary struggle is fleeting, but the glory that comes with the Kingdom of God is forever.

Psalm 33:22

"May your unfailing love be with us, Lord, even as we put our hope in you."

- **The Good News:** God's love is always with us.

Hebrews 13:5-6

"Keep your lives free from the love of money and be content with what you have, because God has said, 'Never will I leave you; never will I forsake you.' So we say with confidence, 'The Lord is my helper; I will not be afraid. What can mere mortals do to me?'"

- **The Good News:** Be content with your circumstances, because no matter how bad things get, God has never forsaken you.

John 14:27

"Peace I leave with you; my peace I give you. I do not give to you as the world gives. Do not let your hearts be troubled and do not be afraid."

- **The Good News:** God gives you peace through his love and understanding.

Psalm 46:10

"He says, 'Be still and know that I am God; I will be exalted among the nations, I will be exalted in the earth.'"

- **The Good News:** Take comfort and peace in God's strength.

Psalm 56:8

"Record my misery; list my tears on your scroll — are they not in your record?"

- **The Good News:** God knows every tear you cry and every struggle you face, and He is with you.

Psalm 147:3

"He heals the brokenhearted and binds up their wounds."

- **The Good News:** God takes care of anyone who is struggling, sad, or hurt.

1 Peter 5:7

"Cast all your anxiety on him because he cares for you."

- **The Good News:** God can handle any amount of anxiety or worry you have, so put it all on Him rather than carrying it all yourself.

Proverbs 23:18

"This is surely a future hope for you, and your hope will not be cut off."

- **The Good News:** With God, there is hope. The future isn't as scary when you think of things this way.

Matthew 6:34

"Therefore do not worry about tomorrow, for tomorrow will worry about itself. Each day has enough trouble of its own."

- **The Good News:** There is no point in worrying about tomorrow. Take things one day at a time.

1 Philippians 4:6-7

"Do not be anxious about anything, but in every situation, by prayer and petition, with thanksgiving, present your requests to God. And the peace of God, which transcends all understanding, will guard your hearts and your minds in Christ Jesus."

- **The Good News:** Instead of worrying about how you will handle everything on your own, put all your worries and anxieties on God, who can handle anything.

2 Timothy 4:17

"But the Lord stood at my side and gave me strength, so that through me the message might be fully proclaimed and all the Gentiles might hear it. And I was delivered from the lion's mouth."

- **The Good News:** God will stand next to you and give you strength in any situation, no matter how daunting.

Psalm 31:24

"Be strong and take heart, all you who hope in the Lord."

- **The Good News:** If you have a relationship with God, then there is hope.

Job 5:11

"The lowly he sets on high, and those who mourn are lifted to safety."

- **The Good News:** God takes care of those who are in low, unsafe places. He comforts and protects them.

John 16:33

"I have told you these things, so that in me you may have peace. In this world you will have trouble. But take heart! I have overcome the world."

- **The Good News:** God sent his only son to die for our sins, so he can do anything. There is no need to worry or stress.

2 Corinthians 1:3

"Praise be to the God and Father of our Lord Jesus Christ, the Father of compassion and the God of all comfort."

- **The Good News:** God is the ultimate giver of compassion, comfort, and strength, so lean on him in times of need.

Psalm 32:7

"You are my hiding place; you will protect me from trouble and surround me with songs of deliverance."

- **The Good News:** Let God be your place of refuge in tough times. He is ever present.

Psalm 40:1

"I waited patiently for the Lord; he turned to me and heard my cry."

- **The Good News:** God will always answer your cries.

Psalm 55:22

Cast your cares on the Lord and he will sustain you; he will never let the righteous be shaken."

- **The Good News:** Whatever worries you face, put them on God. He will never ignore his children.

Psalm 56:3

"When I am afraid, I put my trust in you."

- **The Good News:** Whenever you are afraid, God is where you should put your trust and worries. He will comfort you.

Proverbs 29:25

"Fear of a man will prove to be a snare, but whoever trusts in the Lord is kept safe."

- **The Good News:** Fear can be a downfall for anyone, but trusting in God keeps you protected and safe.

Isaiah 26:3

"You will keep in perfect peace those whose minds are steadfast because they trust you."

- **The Good News:** Trusting in God offers a type of peace that is beyond our human understanding.

Jeremiah 29:11

"'For I know the plans I have for you,' declares the Lord, 'plans to prosper you and not to harm you, plans to give you hope and a future.'"

- **The Good News:** God knows everything about your past, present, and future, and because of this, there is no need to worry.

Made in the USA
Columbia, SC
11 November 2024